So You
Want to
Preach

Frederick Keller Stamm

So You Want to Preach

ABINGDON PRESS NEW YORK • NASHVILLE

SO YOU WANT TO PREACH

Copyright © MCMLVIII by Abingdon Press

Library of Congress Catalog Card Number: 58-8124

SET UP, PRINTED, AND BOUND BY THE
PARTHENON PRESS, AT NASHVILLE,
TENNESSEE, UNITED STATES OF AMERICA

Dedicated To All
Who Bear Glad Tidings
of
Great Joy

FOREWORD

On a few occasions I have been asked to write a book on how to study, how to prepare sermons, and how to preach them. I could never bring myself to do it, for the simple reason that I have known some men who defied all the laws of homiletics, but who were great preachers. And I have known some who were next to perfect in sermon construction, yet who lacked the essentials that make preaching effective. In my own case there has been nothing essentially different in sermon preparation and construction that cannot be duplicated or excelled by hundreds of preachers all over the world.

So this is not a book on how to preach. I am thinking more especially of the broader aspects of preaching, what it ought to mean to the younger generation of preachers and to the waiting congregations. John Keats, the poet, died at twenty-five. One night as he returned from talking with Leigh Hunt at Hampstead, he sat and wrote these exquisite lines, thinking of youth:

And other spirits there are standing apart
  Upon the forehead of the age to come;
These, these will give the world another heart,
And other pulses. Hear ye not the hum
Of mighty workings?—
Listen awhile, ye nations, and be dumb.

Somehow I have been intrigued by the words "standing upon the forehead of the age to come," for that is exactly where the young men in the ministry are standing. I thought as I set down these pages that I might say something which would help them to give this age "another heart, and other pulses."

FREDERICK KELLER STAMM

CONTENTS

1. GETTING STARTED 13

2. PITFALLS FOR THE PREACHER 24

3. THE PROPHET IN THE PULPIT 44

4. THE PRIEST AT THE ALTAR 71

5. MANKIND IS YOUR BUSINESS 91

*So You
Want to
Preach*

GETTING STARTED

1

So you want to preach! Charles E. Jefferson, for thirty-one years the famous preacher of the Broadway Tabernacle, now the Broadway Congregational Church, New York City, entered Harvard University with the expectation of becoming a lawyer. One Sunday morning he went to hear Phillips Brooks preach, then again and again, until, under the skillful handling of the gospel by Brooks, plus his matchless personality—a little child described him as having a face that "looked like the face of Jesus"—Jefferson was impelled to leave the study of law and become a minister. Perhaps still under the spell of Phillips Brooks when he gave the charge to the preacher at my installation in Brooklyn, he said, "A church is here not to make a *show*, but to do a *work*; a preacher is here not to make a *show*, but to do a *work*."

It may be that some such experience has been yours. Perhaps your Godly father and mother, consciously or unconsciously, set your mind and heart in the direction of the ministry. Or one day as you followed the plow or sat in the gloaming of the day, the personality, the whole life and teaching, of Jesus, his manhood and his sonship in God, came to you as it did to my friend Joseph Fort Newton, whose mother said to him, "Listen only to Jesus, accept what he says about God, what he has shown God to be in his life, nothing else, nothing less; test everything by him—forget the rest." It was the glory of this Jesus that filled your being, and it was in the ministry that you could best show him to the world. Or your minister or a friend planted a thought in your heart and mind which sent you to college and on to the seminary. It is possible, too, that you can't give an easily defined reason why you chose the ministry. From childhood to adolescence to maturity you naturally gravitated toward the ministry. You can't tell why; it just seemed the thing to do.

At any rate, whatever it was that constrained you, here you are—a preacher. It is the day you have looked forward to. You are a bit awe-struck with it all. You have your diploma, you have been ordained, and you are set as the minister of a church. Your heart rejoices, and your church is proud of its new young minister. As I look back upon a similar experience, I see you facing joys and sorrows, successes and failures, victories and defeats. As I visualize all this, and much more, I think I would like to invite you into the privacy of my study here in the country where we can sit and chat awhile about the things that are of mutual concern.

You are starting out amidst a world environment which is not much different from the one in which you have been living ever since you were born. You are familiar with the world's tensions. Jet planes, guided missiles, atom bombs, hydrogen bombs, cobalt bombs, are familiar words in your vocabulary. As I write these words, Albert Schweitzer is telling the world in no uncertain terms what particles of Strontium 90 sifting down through the atmosphere will mean to the health of peoples not only now but in later generations. Whether, as our government would like to have us believe, a "clean" bomb will ever be perfected, it is no secret that if nuclear weapons are ever unleashed by the nations, we will have a dirty war, the dirtiest ever. What the future holds, no one is brash enough to predict. But whether God will find another way out depends upon little boys and girls, mature men and women, and I think largely upon the present-day generation of ministers.

But you will have to hurry. There are only two major problems confronting the world—human brotherhood and war and peace. They are like washing one hand with the other. If you clean one, you clean the other. If you know the mind of Jesus, it is simple to discover that it was these two problems that concerned him. Read again the account of the temptation, the Sermon on the Mount, and almost any one of his great parables. They were the concern of Jefferson and Lincoln and a host of like-minded thinkers ever since the dawn of civilization. It has been the disciplined and consecrated hearts and minds of great men and women who have pointed the path down which the world can walk toward the City of God. I shall have more to say as to your contribution to the solution of these problems, but just now, with the instruments of self-destruction in men's hands for the first time in history, in the language of Christopher Fry in *A Sleep of Prisoners,*

> Thank God our time is now when wrong
> Comes up to face us everywhere,
> Never to leave us till we take
> The longest stride of soul men ever took.
> Affairs are now soul size.
> . . . .
> Good is itself, what ever comes.
> It grows, and makes, and bravely
> Persuades, beyond all tilt of wrong:
> Stronger than anger, wiser than strategy,
> Enough to subdue cities and men
> If we believe it with a long courage of truth.[1]

The normal expectancy of your ministry is thirty, forty, or even fifty years. Living in an age that moves more rapidly than ever before, the shape of things to come in your lifetime will be enough to dazzle the wildest imagination. So instead of pontificating as though I know all the answers to the problems which you will face and along the path which your generation will pass, I shall talk about things as I see them and about some old truths of God and man which will be true for you as they have been true for me and as they have been true forever. It is the

[1] Used by permission of Oxford University Press.

old truths adapted to meet new conditions which have spoken to the experiences of men down through history and which have lighted the dusty path for many a weary pilgrim.

I do not want to talk with you about the doctrines of the church or its dogmas. You have been instructed in the classroom, read books, and have learned what churchmen have held as to these things from the beginning of the Christian era. I do not ask you either to bind them to your breast with bands of steel or to throw them out of the window. I have sat where you recently sat. I learned much of what you have been learning. But I had to ask myself, Is this true? Will it stand the test, not with the credulous folk who want to be told what to believe, but among folk who through suffering, mental anguish, and spiritual experience want to move out into the light of God where they can find him closer than breathing and nearer than hands and feet? Is it the authority of the church expressed in creed and dogma which will save the world, or is it the mature mind lighted by the presence of a God of understanding and love for all peoples whether friendly or antagonistic?

No, I do not want to talk with you about creeds, doctrines, and dogmas, much as they seem to be of influence in holding the church together, much as you may lean on them in your extremity for lack of something better, and much as I may feel at times the need of stability rather than some nebulus idea of God which can only spell confusion and uncertainty in the man or woman who wants something solid underfoot.

17

You yourself must decide your creedal position, and other men must be your champions in behalf of the doctrines handed down from age to age through the church. I would talk to you about practical things which will meet you along the road you will have to walk. They will bob out at you around the corner, in unexpected places, along the hill called Difficulty and in the Valley of Humiliation. They will sneak up on you when you are not looking for them, in hours when your spirits are low, and in the days of your greatest triumph.

They will be there because your main business is the imperial souls of men. People in other businesses and professions do not see them and are not troubled by them, not because they are impervious to the wistfulness, the loneliness, and the despair of thousands of human beings, but because their main interests lie in other directions. Perhaps this is as it should be or is inevitable. We look to a multitude of men to provide us with food, clothing, homes, railroads, airplanes, automobiles, and what not. One would hardly be justified in saying that these men are callous to human need. Some are, and it is possible that there are more than we imagine. But we are blind if we have never seen men who are not. They are not without the milk of human kindness. Their so-called secular enterprises may be as sacred as that of the preacher in the pulpit or the priest at the altar.

Even so, their specialty is not the preacher's specialty. The church is not an iron curtain behind which the preacher can hide and within whose confines he can keep

18

his hands from becoming soiled with the affairs of the world. While he may well thank God for the opportunity of seeing things with a clearer vision than the man who sits in the pew, yet all the joys and sorrows, victories and defeats of men; all the sordidness, wickedness, and diabolism, as well as the love, kindness, and forgiveness of mankind, are laid at his doorstep. He can't very well turn away from all this with a shrug of the shoulder. It is his problem simply because he chose the ministry and because his main concern is not his study, his beautiful church, or the club to which he belongs, but out where cross the crowded ways of life.

Not everything I say will be the truth, the *whole* truth. I know only a segment of the truth, and some things I believe to be true may not be true at all. But it is along the path toward truth that every minister should walk; and if, as years pass, he finds a new light breaking upon his pathway, he would better discard the old and grapple with the new. In any event, I trust you are not going to preach with the idea that you must present an argument in behalf of Christlikeness. The religion you declare is not a debate but a life. In Jesus you have seen what life really is when it is lived fearlessly, faithfully, and abundantly, in obedience to the law of God and the universe. If you have caught one little glimpse of him and made his life your own, you know what religion is from the inside, how it works, and its power. John's Gospel calls him the Light, and the testimony of the ages is that there is a glory in his bosom that transfigures you and me. When that happens, we become willing and worthy transmitters of that Light.

The old mystics had it right, as have had all the light bringers from the beginning of time. They did not argue; they let in the light. To them religion is a tie that binds God and man together where "Spirit with Spirit can meet." George Fox said that though he read about God and Christ, he knew them only when he had a soul like theirs, else they could not be known at all. He knew that to know the truth we ourselves must become truth; it must first be lived, and out of a luminous life must come luminous thinking.

If, as you set out on your ministry, all the mysteries of life, sin, sorrow, and death have not yet made their impact upon your soul, the better you know the Man who gave his life that light might shine into the dark places of men's lives, the clearer will light on these things break upon your path. If you think at all and ponder upon the thing that causes countless thousands to mourn, that wrings the cry of pain and misery from the lips of God's children all around the world, and that spills innocent blood of millions of men, women, and children through cruel and insane war, you will not take light views of sin. You may call it by any name you wish, "missing the mark" and what not, it is still sin, and no rose-water sentiment can disinfect it. You may be sure as you read the literature of the ages that no great masters and interpreters of the soul ever made light of it. Shakespeare saw it in all its terrifying effects. Socrates saw it as the result of ignorance. Plato looked deeper when he said that at the bottom of the

20

mind is a sediment, something stupid, which, when stirred by passion, befogs the reason and blinds it. Men become like wild horses and drag the chariot of life to wreckage. What Socrates left dark, Plato lighted up. It remained for Aristotle to tell us that at the center of all morality is the will, and until we reckon with the profound perversity of the will which destroys rather than restores, lies when convenient, kills the reputation of good men, despoils freedom of speech and press, and makes our boasted Christianity a laughingstock, we have not yet measured the thing called sin.

But this is only half the truth. Great as is the light thrown upon sin by the Greek thinkers, none of them tells us how to get rid of it. With them it remains a riddle. Reason does not supply the remedy. Only that which stands above reason can reach down to sin, deal with it, and melt it away. Here on the darkest path a mortal ever trod and in a Person whose life seemed to end in a bottomless pit is the light that is sorely needed. The only way you can see what sin is is to set it against the background of the white life of Jesus. The forgiving, suffering, cleansing love of the Cross is the beacon light in an otherwise hopeless night. If that light fails, no other power can win, and the soul of man and the world goes on to a fate which is horrible to predict.

But I should not like to ring down the curtain here on the note of *sin*. Nor should I like to see you start out with the idea that the main emphasis of your ministry should be upon sin. Somehow we have had strange notions about re-

21

ligion. We have thought that God goes peering into the lives of people, sees the wrong that lurks in them, and then threatens them with dire punishment if they do not mend. But that was not the way of Jesus. He did something better than to call men vile sinners. He went about drawing out and encouraging the exercise of what was already in his fellow men. To the cripple he said, "You can walk. You have the power." And the man got to his feet at the command and walked. To those in the boat, fearful of the storm, he said, "Be not afraid. Exercise your faith." To the woman who tremblingly touched the hem of his garment he said, "Your faith has made you whole." To the tax collector he said, "You are not as bad as people say you are. There is goodness within you. Let it out. Use it." And the man made a new start. Nobody thought publicans were lovable—nobody but Jesus. No one thought Martha or Matthew or Thomas particularly prepossessing—they appeared quite ordinary and featureless with no distinctive talents or social gifts. No one but Jesus thought them amazingly lovable. No one could have been more surprised than these lonely people themselves. They did not know. But he knew, and knowing, he brought out the best in them. A word from Jesus was a mirror in which everyone could look and see a nobler self. How gentle, how strong, how unwearying, is the love that will not let us go, bearing all things, believing all things, hoping all things!

What a challenge to you! What a privilege is yours of letting the love of God shine into the hearts of men and women and little children! What an opportunity to restore to men and women their faith in life and in the value of its struggle! This must forever be the redeeming, healing force in the world. When darkness becomes light in the lives of those whom you serve, you are making little Christs in the interest of the world's redemption.

PITFALLS FOR THE PREACHER

2

A FEW YEARS AFTER HAVING BEEN GRADUATED FROM THE seminary, a well-known preacher with whom I had become acquainted and who was more than a friend to me until the day he died said to me, "You got a good foundation at that little seminary." All through the years I have cherished a profound respect and love for the professors who set my feet in the direction of a sane and rational concept of religion. It kept me from running off at tangents and preserved me from an emotionalism which has neither rhyme nor reason in setting men's feet in the pathway that leads to God.

I never had any emotional upheaval in my religious experience. What I got in college and seminary was the thing for which I had been looking from my boyhood days, but which I could not put into words. It was a liberal outlook upon religion and life. It was not a humanism which left no room for the operation of the spirit of

God upon the spirit of man, nor yet a dogmatism which demanded belief in man-made doctrines. Jesus was not a side issue, the Cross only a symbol, and ritual the paramount concern of the preacher. Jesus and his prophetic utterances, his hope for a kingdom of righteousness, his emphasis upon love for God and man, his desire for a new way of life, and his love of freedom from anything that smacked of dogmatism have all led me down a path in which I have loved to walk; and I could wish that I might live long enough to see Jesus put where he belongs—at the center of our ecclesiastical, political, and international life. My patron saint has been not Martin Luther, but Erasmus, who hoped to take religion out of the hands of the theologians and put it into the hands of Jesus, where it belongs. Unfortunately the church as a whole is not too well acquainted with nor does it have any great desire to catch the spirit of Erasmus.

Having said this, however, I find myself wishing that I had known more about human relations when I entered the ministry and that somewhere in the curriculum of the seminary there had been a course telling me how to deal with all sorts of people and situations in the church and how not to set myself up as an authority in all things ecclesiastical and religious. As I have visited seminaries and come into contact with any number of young and older ministers, and watched assistants trying to make their way, I have wished that they too had been better equipped to meet the exacting demands of a life that throws them into the midst of humanity's stream where saints and sinners

25

alike play at making the church a repository of the spirit of God. There are pitfalls for the preacher, and although falling into them may not spell his utter ruin, they reduce his effectiveness and make him only the semblance of a man who can command the respect of the so-called pagan and the avowed Christian.

I trust I shall not appear pedantic when I say that the first pit into which the young preacher can fall is the lack of mental and spiritual discipline. The first business of a preacher is to preach, and if he doesn't want to do that, he would better seek another vocation. Preaching is a lifetime job, and when a man of my age looks back, he says to himself, "I wish I had been better able to speak to the experiences of men than I have been." Times without number I have looked upon fellow preachers and said, "I wish I could ring the changes on the gospel as they can." But I did hope from the beginning that I could become an acceptable preacher.

The complaint I have heard all my life has been that no church wants a preacher after he is forty-five. No one needs to fool himself with the belief that all pulpit committees are intelligent in their selection of a minister. Anyone who has had occasion to observe the workings of the minds of committees in this respect must have wondered what manner of men and women they were. All too many ecclesiastical disasters have been caused by committees that had little knowledge as to the quality of the man they were selecting and what a preacher is for.

But where one mistake of this kind has been made, there are a dozen preachers complaining that they had not been chosen for a particular pulpit. Churchmen frequently have an uncanny sense of the fitness of things and can usually detect how far a preacher has gone in his thinking, whether he has kept his mind alert or whether he has reached a dead end. Many a man has preached himself out long before he has reached forty-five, and if he spends the balance of his days complaining that he has been set aside for a younger man, if he examines himself, he may find that it is not his age but the sterility of his mind. There are preachers who are young at sixty and others who are old and spiritually blind at thirty. Every minister is his own boss, and he can idle away his time if he chooses. Preaching itself is comparatively easy; the thing that is hard is getting ready to preach. At best a preacher is only a child picking up pebbles on the shores of knowledge. It takes all the stuff there is in him even down to old age. But he would better die now than reach the place where power has gone out of him and where he fails to sing the Lord's song with joy and gladness of heart. Any young man can avoid this pitfall if he sets out to love God, not only with his heart, but also with his mind.

It is not far from sterility of mind to the pitfall of wanting his own *way* instead of his *say*. It is so easy for a preacher to become frustrated when it dawns on him that not all the people give full response to what he conceives to be the gospel. The fact is that his preaching may be a long sea mile from the truth. Maybe he is sowing chaff instead of good grain, so how can he expect a harvest? Maybe what he is preaching is not good news at all. Failing to recognize his own lack of spiritual insight, he be-

27

comes frustrated; and when that happens, it is not long before he is accusing everyone else for lack of spiritual discernment and for their refusal to regard the preacher as an expert in all things ecclesiastical.

In the light of history one would be a fool to declare that congregations everywhere hang upon every word that the noble and well-equipped preacher utters, or that they like their prejudices and preconceived notions of religion disturbed, whether from the pulpit or in the general administration of the church. Many a gallant preacher's heart has been broken by some hard-fisted officers who thought the church belonged to them, or by some racially prejudiced congregation, or by an ultrapious individual who thought he was in possession of the faith once delivered to the saints.

During my earliest ministry when the way was sometimes very hard, I read newspaper and magazine accounts of the success of preachers in metropolitan pulpits and thought how wonderful it must be to have large congregations looking up into the preacher's face, waiting upon his inspiring word, and following his leadership. Later I became acquainted with a number of these men, sat in conversation with them, and preached in their pulpits. I saw the lines on their faces, felt the wounds in their hearts, and learned of their disillusionments. They were more than "men of the cloth"; they were men after God's own heart. I saw a few of them depart from their pulpits brokenhearted at a comparatively early age, take another church, and die in a few years.

No, I would not be so rash as to say that all church

28

troubles stem from the preacher. I wish there had been, and would be now, more preachers such as those written about in an article in *Harper's* magazine under the title "The Churches Repent," by Lee Nichols and Louis Cassels. It is the story of both Protestant preachers and Roman Catholic priests who had to fight the battle for racial integration in their churches and how some succeeded and some were defeated. Increasingly it will take that kind of preacher to make the church Christlike. Nor would I say that at no time does a church board need the severe criticism of the preacher. I got it firsthand from a preacher friend who knew that in a historic church in this country two noted pulpiteers were heckled to the point of distraction and utter discouragement by the officers. Shortly after the call of a third man he walked into the monthly meeting of his officials one evening, seated himself, put his feet on the table, looked around upon the assembled men and said, "I hear you are a bunch of butchers in this church. I just thought I would like to say that if there is to be any killing, I'd like to have a hand in it myself." Perhaps a smile played about his lips as he said those words, but the import of them was no less effective, and he carried on a splendid ministry for many years. I got it also firsthand that another preacher said one morning, "I wish many of you would not come to church but let me fill the pews with people who want religion." A preacher would better know his ground before following in the footsteps of these two men, and be prepared to take the consequences. But he would better take the consequences rather than lose his own soul.

29

It is difficult to believe, however, that instances of this kind are characteristic of the church. Pulpits are made for men of conviction and with the love of truth in their hearts. But a preacher who uses the precious time in a church worship for the purpose of "laying it on" and thrusting the sword of denunciation into tender hearts and taking his frustration out upon an unsuspecting people will soon find himself on the way out. And when he is out, instead of examining himself, he justifies his self-righteousness while regarding all the people he preached to as wreckers of the house of God, that man has fallen into a pit out of which only the grace and humility of God can lift him.

A preacher is an interpreter, not a dictator and not the special guardian of men's morals. Blessed is the preacher who opens the way of life for men as best he can and then allows them to choose to follow it or not. If I were a non–church member, I would run as fast as I could from the preacher who set out to capture me for Christ. From this terrible superegotism of the preacher who wants to do me good for his own satisfaction and who adopts the attitude "Come and be as I am," good Lord, deliver me! Emerson said, "God knows and I know, that one person in the world like myself is enough." Personally I have never considered myself as the guardian of men's morals, nor do I think it necessary to go about with a strained expression on my countenance and with a determined effort to do my reluctant fellows good or to "hang," as Leslie Weatherhead says, "the scalps of a lot of lovable pagans at my belt." I suspect, too, that there are any number of people in any community who are irked by an official visit from the nearby church in an effort to get them to "join up."

I think if Jesus were here, he would be the kind of person who would be glad when people wanted to tell him their troubles. But I can't think of him as making friends with rich or poor to do them good or to get them to come to church. Nor can I think of him as wanting to pry into people's secrets. I am thinking of him, however, as wanting to make friends with people for friendship's sake and because he was a friendly person, not for any ulterior motive. As Dick Sheppard of St. Martin's-in-the-Fields said, "It is not my business to make people good. It is my business to make myself good, and other people happy if I can." If I were giving one last bit of counsel to any young preacher, it would be, "Just let your light shine into the dark places of men's lives, and if that does not change them, nothing else will."

Here let me say a word about the pitfall into which you may fall if you fail the people in your parish in illness or when death visits a home. Let us pass by the fact that there are people in every church who will not notify you of their illness and then will chide you for not visiting them. These are the exceptions, and no man's ministry will suffer because he is not clairvoyant enough to divine someone's illness. For the most part you will know when people are ill and most certainly when death strikes, and you can depend upon it that people are never so sensitive as at times such as these. What you do or fail to do in these circumstances will bind the hearts of the sufferers to you and the church in lasting devotion and friendship or drive them into indifference, if not hostility.

There is nothing you can do to alleviate the physical suffering, and perhaps there is little you can say to the man or woman who is the victim of an incurable disease. Indeed, words ofttimes are poor vehicles by which to express your sympathy and concern. Much talk and especially pious and emotional prayers only make the sick person wish you would never come again. But a radiant personality can light up the dark places of the sickroom, bring hope in hours of despair, and turn an otherwise hideous night into a waiting for a better day tomorrow.

There is little, too, you can say at the time of death, especially when it comes suddenly and unexpectedly. I could give you any number of personal experiences in this respect, but let only one suffice. A middle-aged woman's husband was dying of cancer. All I could do was to stand by with an occasional short prayer of comfort. Then a month before her twenty-year-old son was to return from army service, he was drowned. What then? Who knows but that in the early days of your ministry you will be confronted with a catastrophe such as that? If you are not flabbergasted and if you do not breathe a prayer to God to show you what to do, you will have different feelings than I had with years of experience behind me.

I had gone to the woman's home a number of times during her husband's illness and officiated at his funeral. When the first telegram came saying that her son might have been drowned, I went to the home, then again, and waited with her until the final dread word came. Much of the time there were few words spoken, and I didn't tarry long. Her eyes were dry, and she concealed her broken heart with a sickly smile.

Then one day as I was walking along the street, her car pulled up to the curb, the door opened, and she invited me in. There in the car the floodwaters broke and she poured out her grief. When it was spent, she said, "Thank you for letting me cry and for your comfort," although I had hardly spoken a word. I got out of the car, she smiled, waved good-by, and drove away.

All your people will want of you when life tumbles in for them is to be a friend who stands by and understands. It is not so much that they want your words as that they want *you*. If you fail them, you need not be surprised if confidence is lost and a friendship spoiled.

Then, too, the preacher who fails to recognize his limitations will fall into the pit of disgruntlement with the world, the church, and himself. Ambition is not a sin, but when his ambition takes the form of jealousy and envy, and he wishes that he might stand in the other man's shoes, that preacher has never acquired the grace of humility and self-effacement which are required for setting a man in line with the truly great spiritual leaders of the past and the present. Nor is it a sin to be a run-of-the-mine preacher. Joseph Fort Newton once told me that someone said that Cadman should never write and Newton should never preach. One can understand what was meant when one remembers the preaching of the one and the writing of the other. But when a man thinks more highly of himself than he ought to think and regards himself as better

33

qualified to occupy a certain pulpit than two thirds of the preachers around him, you can be sure that while he will continue to have the name of a minister, his ministry will be directed largely toward fostering his own ambition.

It has always struck me as a strange and unholy attitude on the part of any number of preachers that they seem to take delight in the fact that the breath of scandal has touched some preacher in the community who has been successful. For example, I recall from my younger years how a falsehood had been told about a neighboring minister in a large parish. It began as a comparatively trivial matter, then magnified to the point where a woman in the church was reported to have given birth to a child which belonged to the minister. I met him one morning on my way to a meeting of the ministers. "Do you know why I attend this meeting?" he asked. Before I could reply, he said, "To keep from being talked about." And it was so. One morning in his absence I asked, "What do we know about this scandal?"

"Oh, nothing," was the reply—"only what we hear."

"Too bad, isn't it," someone remarked, "that a brother minister sixty years of age should be the subject of our gossip, especially on such tenuous evidence? How many of us have gone to him, put a brotherly hand on his shoulder, and said, 'We'll stand by and see you through'?" The gossip hadn't a leg to stand on, it soon passed, and the minister continued to serve that church until his death.

I've often thought that his weathering of the storm was due, not to any encouragement or sympathy on the part of any one of us, but to his own magnificent courage.

Francis of Assisi was once asked, "What would you do if you knew you were going to die on the morrow?" He replied, "I would just go on digging in my own garden." "Digging in their garden" is just what all ministers ought to be doing. Every preacher has his own battles to fight and enough to do to keep his own garden clean without glorying in another man's failures or being jealous of his successes. There are little men in the ministry with little minds and little hearts, and if they remain nonentities, it is not the fault of the church or because they have been discriminated against, but because they are more concerned about another man's garden than their own. No man can help his lack of mental ability, but he can keep from looking at life and his brothers in a little way. Any preacher can select the qualities he should like to have and then act as if he had them. He can set himself some high standards and try to live up to them.

One of the joys of my boyhood days was sitting under a young man who had just come from the seminary to our little village church. I was confirmed by him at the age of twelve and rarely missed a Sunday church service. I do not remember anything he said, but I remember him. When he left our church, he took another rural church, then later a small mission church which grew into a thriving congregation with a new church building. No one ever called him a great preacher, but he preached as well as he could. Nor could anyone say he was without ambition, but his ambition was to do his work well wherever he was. In his later years I saw him occasionally, and I never forgot to pay my respects to him and to tell him what he had meant to me as a young lad. He died at eighty, and when his family asked me to preach his memorial sermon, I called him a saint, for he was all that—and more. There was nothing spectacular about him, never wanting a place he could not fill; he was just a plain man doing a job at the place where he was set down. I bow in reverence before men of that kind all over the country and with qualities I may well covet for myself. All of us could well make the parable of the talents a daily study.

Another pitfall for the preacher is that of setting himself up as an economic expert. Now and then a man, such as Norman Thomas, appears who finds it necessary to leave the parish ministry and direct his efforts in the field of politics and economics, or such as a young man I knew many years ago who came back from the foreign field and applied his religion in behalf of the soft coal miners in the United States. I honor men of this kind. We owe them a debt we can never pay. Besides, a man is not necessarily a turncoat if he leaves the parish for some other work. Perhaps he belongs where he has gone, and it is conceivable that he can do more there in the interest of the kingdom of God than we who stick to our first love. Maybe, too, a number of misfits in the ministry would do well to seek other vocations.

Most of us, however, succeed only in making ourselves look ridiculous and losing the respect of high-thinking laymen in the church when we try to identify a particular economic system with the kingdom of God. Regardless of our adherence to one system or another, they all have their faults, and by no stretch of the imagination can we think of

Jesus as throwing his influence in favor of any one of them. But we can think of Jesus with his wholesome respect for human personality and his belief in man's integrity as saying to all men everywhere, "O that thou hadst hearkened to my commandments! then had thy peace been as a river, and thy righteousness as the waves of the sea." We can think of him as saying that no system is worth a picayune in the long run that does not put human life above every other consideration. For taking this position, a preacher's reputation might be as completely destroyed as was the body of Jesus when his God-consciousness came into conflict with the prevailing political and ecclesiastical opinion of his day. But it would be worth it.

Despite the fact that the social gospel of forty-five years ago got lost in the midst of two wars, a depression, and a theology that says only God can do anything, man is a vile sinner and can do nothing by way of making the world better, there is still a social gospel—still the demand that capital and labor, rich man and poor man, king and peasant, preacher and people, shall do justly, love mercy, and walk humbly before God. Take that out of family life, economic life, personal, national, and international life, and the whole structure goes to pieces. I've lived long enough to hear corroborated by many industrial leaders what many of us preached years ago, that he to whom much is given, of him is much required. Wise-minded industrialists are saying today that much of the trouble between capital and labor has been due to the high-handed methods of industry, and have set about to correct them.

Let the preacher wrap up his message in a neat little

37

theological formula if he wishes to do so. But if he does, he will be doing less than a tinker's job. Or let him drive hard in the direction of setting up an economic Utopia which he thinks is the last authoritative word, and he will find his congregation diminishing, his people losing confidence in him, and his gospel without substance. But let him take his stand where the prophets and Jesus stood—in the hearts of people who long for a better day, who know mercy, justice, and righteousness when they see them lived—and though some storms may swirl about his head, his integrity, honesty, urgency, and sound thinking will yet be recognized, and the people will say, "What else is the preacher for but to lead us into the way of justice, mercy, and truth?" If the preacher, instead of upsetting the applecart and running off in a hundred different directions at once the moment he steps into a new parish, would first gain the confidence of his people, he would not be wading about so much of the time in hot water, consulting the yearbook, filing his application with the denominational supply committee, or sitting on the bishop's doorstep with the hope of finding another pulpit.

What, finally, should I say about the manner of treatment that should be accorded by the preacher to his predecessor, to the old man who is now retired? I have known all too many preachers who were never completely accepted by their people all because they lacked common courtesy, or Christian grace, or psychological sense, in this respect. Personally I have never had occasion to complain about any real or imaginary discourtesy on the part of any of my successors. I pity any man who is so thick-skinned as never to feel a hurt. I am about as sensitive to hurt as a mortal man can be, but in my case I have always been too far removed or too busy in various directions to meddle in the affairs of my successor or to criticize him because he has another way of handling his parish than I had. No two persons are alike, and every man must win his spurs in his own way.

There are, however, meddlesome old preachers who never learned how to keep their hands off the helm of the church once they have left it. The retired minister would better say to himself, "I have had my day; let the other man have his." On the contrary, the newly appointed minister will live in misery if he magnifies the ill effect upon his work should the former minister return to perform a ministerial function, or should the retired predecessor, who settles in the community, baptize a baby, officiate at a wedding, or bury an old friend.

It never dawned upon me that any man who preceded me could injure me or my work, or that I should be unduly exercised if he attempted to. I have never yet known how to change the natural or acquired disposition of a seventy-year-old man, preacher or layman, but I am sure there is a way to keep from flying at his throat, and how to play the part of a mature man instead of that of a badly spoiled child.

As quite a young man I was called to a downtown city church to succeed a man who had been there for forty years. Everybody in the city seemed to know him; he had many friends and some violent enemies. Preachers said, "I pity your having to step into the old man's shoes. He will make life miserable for you." Then one day we talked together, and I found him to be a man of parts and a delightful personality, and I was drawn to him. In the course of our conversation I said to him, "You have been here a long time. You have many friends, and I want you to keep them. No doubt some will want you at a baptism, a wedding, or funeral, and if so, please be free to minister to them." The old man's eyes filled with tears, and he thanked me. He baptized a few children, married a few couples, and buried a few friends. That was the end. He never did a discourteous thing, and he pointed me in some good directions.

I stand amazed as I see the arrogance and the egotism of some young preachers. For example, I knew a preacher who served a church for thirty-five years. When he took the church, it had a small membership and an inadequate building. When he retired at seventy-five, there was a large membership and a much enlarged and beautified edifice, and no debt. He never received a salary of more than 3,500 dollars and lived in an unrenovated manse all that time. The new man was set down in the midst of a thriving congregation, a greatly increased salary—as it should have been—and a manse completely renovated. The old minister came to the end of his ministry with little financial security for the future, no house of his own, only the semblance of a pension, and a pitiable monthly stipend from the church. I knew him through the years, and the finest tribute I ever heard paid a man came from a citizen of the community who said to me, "I never knew a man who talked so little religion and lived so much of it as he."

Yet one day when the new young minister was settled in the parish, he said to the old man, "You and I are two different men, and I would be obliged if you would not interfere." The old man was not the kind who would interfere with anyone, and no man knew better than he that one man labors and another enters into his labors; but I knew when I talked with him that he did not feel at home when he went to the church into which he had put thirty-five sacrificial years, all because there was an ungracious host in the house of the Lord.

There is an elderly retired preacher in New York by the name of John Haynes Holmes whose fame as a preacher has gone far beyond his own parish. By the orthodox he is considered a heretic. If Rufus Jones was right in his book *The Church's Debt to Heretics*, one wonders what would have become of the church had it not been for the heretics. When as a young man I was living in the city of Dayton, Ohio, Holmes came to my church to preach, and ever since I have counted him as a friend and learned much from him I would not have known otherwise. When I had lunch with him one day in New York a few years ago, he fell to reminiscing about his forty years in that city and told me that on his last day there some prominent men had come to the church and said some nice things about him and his work. At the dinner table that evening in his home a few friends whom he had invited continued to praise his work over that long span of years. "My wife," he said, "who could always deflate my ego, listened and finally said,

41

'I do not know why you are saying all these nice things about my husband. He has been preaching on that same corner, lo, these forty years, and instead of the world growing better, it has grown steadily worse.'" I thought as he related this incident how little lesser men than he contribute to the kingdom of God. So why should the spirit of mortal man be proud?

When we sat together that evening after he spoke in my church in Dayton, I told him I had just finished reading his biography of Robert Collyer, who was called the "Anvil Preacher" because he had been a blacksmith, and who had acquired his education by reading and studying all the volumes of the *Encyclopaedia Britannica*. Holmes's eyes could twinkle, and his powers of description could not be excelled. So he told me many things about the "Anvil Preacher," among them this, which every preacher may well lay on his heart and which I could wish every student in every theological seminary could know: "When I became the successor to Dr. Collyer in the church in New York," he said, "I was a young man and with a gospel quite different from his. He was growing old and was not well and walked with a cane. Every Sunday I had a chair reserved for him on the pulpit platform. It was his right, and I wanted him to occupy it. There he sat every Sunday he was able to be present. If he wanted to take part in the service of the morning, he was at liberty to do so. I always knew how the sermon struck him. If he liked it, he would grasp my hand and say so. If he didn't like it, he would stomp past me, down the aisle, and out of the

42

church without a word to me or anyone else. The old man and I hit it off beautifully together."

When the minister becomes so pompous, so sure of himself, so certain that his administration of the church is the best ever devised and his preaching superior to that of every other man, let him retire to his closet and remember that his way is made easier, the fields riper for the harvest, because someone before him prepared the soil and sowed the seed. But further than that, Jesus surprised people with his goodness. His life was different from any they had ever known. It was better than they had ever dreamed one man's life could be. If the church has lost this element of surprise at goodness, I could hope it would regain it in the present generation of preachers. It will if you are the kind of men who can look out over the horizon with a deep sense of your own littleness and yet have faith, hope, and love. If you know that every man is as noble, as vile, as divine, and as lonely as you are, and if you learn to forgive and love your fellows. If you know that every day is a little life, every night a little death, and that you pass this way but once in your journey.

THE PROPHET IN THE PULPIT

3

WHEN WOODROW WILSON MADE HIS LAST SPEECH IN DEFENSE of the League of Nations at Pueblo, Colorado, and just before he was stricken with paralysis, he said, "My *clients* are the children; my *clients* are the future generations."

We may be able to accomplish a few things in a lifetime, but not many. We are like the runners in the ancient torch races—we go so far and then hand the torch to another and he to still another. This is the way with all imperishables. Only as we live with the end in view that our small contribution will light the way to something more significant, are we justified in living at all.

Someone asked long ago, "What difference would it make if all of us had our heads chopped off in the next five minutes?" Not much if our aim is self-glorification. But a great deal if the clients for whom we speak and work are the children and the future generations. Ours

44

is the generation which Woodrow Wilson was trying to save. The question is, Will we carry on where he left off?

No one worth his salt as a minister will be so much of a fool as to imagine that he has spoken the last word on anything that vitally affects the weal or woe of the human soul, or that spells the salvation or damnation of the world. But no man who presumes to be a spokesman for God can hope to escape the judgment of his fellows and his listening congregation as to his sincerity, honesty, insight into truth, and his desire to come to grips with the profoundest principles of religion.

It was my privilege to hear Washington Gladden only once. But one day in Columbus, Ohio, I walked into his church to see where this great prophet held forth for so many years and to breathe the atmosphere of a sanctuary which resounded with the strains of "O Master, Let Me Walk with Thee." As I was talking one day with an Episcopal clergyman and a fellow townsman of Gladden's, he said to me, "I never knew a preacher with such deep insight into spiritual truth as has Washington Gladden. No man is a greater interpreter of the gospel."

Awhile later a young preacher—a bit older than I—called on me at my home. When I learned his name and that he lived in Columbus, I remarked, "It must be a privilege to live in the same city with Washington Gladden and sometimes to sit at his feet and listen."

"Oh," he replied, "he has no standing in Columbus. He is little short of an unbeliever. I wouldn't go across the street to hear him."

All I could do was to exclaim, "Oh!" I felt sorry for

45

him, not because he was obviously steeped in literalism, but because his mind was closed to anything that came from one of America's great preachers. If a young man refuses to allow his mind to roam the universe in search of the great truths of life, his soul will grow narrow, the Bible will become a book only of plaster saints instead of living, struggling, sinning, conquering men and women, and his preaching will eventually sputter out like a spent coal.

The ministry is no place for a closed mind. There are great truths awaiting your discovery, and when you find them, they will create a passion in your preaching, and your people will feel that somehow the man in the pulpit knows God and life and man. So I hope as you start out to preach, you will want to speak a sure word to the congregation that sits at your feet every Sunday morning and that the word you speak will have enough truth in it that the people will know you are speaking, not only to them, but to their children and their children's children.

I am not concerned here with marshaling scripture passages on the nature of the prophetic function of your ministry. The Old Testament is alive with them, and you may be sure that Jesus and the New Testament writers were not speaking for their day alone. If that were true, the Bible would have long since become a lost book. If you are a searcher for the profundities and imperishables with which they and other men have dealt down through the ages, you will find them. More than that, you will deal with them and regard most other things as side issues. There is one prophet, however, not so well known as the great writing prophets such as Isaiah, Jeremiah, Amos, and Hosea, but who had their courage and instinct, and who sounded the note for all who court something other than popularity. It was Micaiah in the days of Ahab and Jezebel in Israel. When the messenger arrived to summon Micaiah into the presence of Ahab, he told Micaiah that the four hundred prophets of Baal were predicting good for Ahab if he should fight the battle of Ramoth-gilead, and added, "Let thy word, I pray thee, be like the word of one of them, and speak that which is good." But Micaiah could not follow that advice. He was under another compulsion: "As the Lord liveth, what the Lord saith unto me, that will I speak."

Henry Thoreau said that if he didn't march with the crowd, it was because he heard a different drummer. So it was with Micaiah. He had gone down into the deeps where the human soul stands face to face with truth. He was sure of himself because he was sure he had hold of a truth bigger than himself. It wasn't that he held some belief about God, but that God held him in his grip. He heard more than the drumbeats on the battlefield of Ramoth-gilead. He heard the beat of the pursuing feet of God against the scheme of death which Ahab was about to launch. He was moving in a moral universe, and that universe was coming into conflict with the kind of universe that leaders such as Ahab always live in. When Gandhi was assassinated, any number of political leaders and newspaper editors extolled him in high terms, but precious few of them, plus any number of preachers, have believed sufficiently in his moral universe to try to live in it. "He that dwelleth in the secret place of the most High" doesn't ring any bells in the hearts of the modern Ahabs.

A prophet such as Micaiah wasn't interested in majorities. If I read the autobiography of Harry Emerson Fosdick aright, I am sure that when he went to Montclair, New Jersey, his first interest was, not how many people he could attract by his preaching, but how near he could come to declaring a truth that would meet human need, point the way down which folk could walk hand in hand with a good God, and how much of God's light he could make break upon the human soul. I am sure, too, that even amidst his trembling whenever he entered the pulpit, his heart was strangely warmed, not merely because crowds swarmed to hear him at the Riverside Church and millions waited upon his radio ministry, but because through the whole wide world men and women rejoiced and came alive through the reading of his books. Who of us could not wish that so many would wait on our ministry and that our influence could be felt far beyond our own parish?

The unfortunate thing is that crowds have also flocked to the conventionally religious preachers, to those who cast their sermons in pious terminology, who register public opinion, and who are moved by surface impulses. They have a religion that adorns, not restrains, that is without any bite and decidedly pleasant because it gives sanction to anything that sovereign might wants to do. It doesn't take much of a preacher to have that kind of religion, and it doesn't take much of a man to want the approval of the "yes men" rather than be fortified by a higher power.

If we know anything about the history of religion, we know that its glory has always been found in those men who were creatures, not of the earth only, but of the sky. Against the corruption of medieval Italy stand Savonarola and Dante. It was not Voltaire and Rousseau who brought an aroused public conscience against the crass materialism of England, but the preaching of John Wesley and the statesmanship of Lord Shaftesbury. Nor will the world ever get out of debt to Frederick Robertson of Brighton and Phillips Brooks of Boston. Men such as these throw a shaft of light that marks a straight path along which generations can move. It is not the sophistries of politicians and diplomats that stir the laggard moral strength of peoples, but the prophets who in the midst of indecision and confusion lift up the great loyalties which command the allegiance of our minds.

I am well aware of the fact that the beginning of many a man's ministry has been spoiled by churches whose unspiritual officials have presumed to guide the spiritual estate of the church, and by irreconcilable quarreling among church groups. But I know also that churches that have wanted to be helpful and co-operative have often found preachers with terrible northeastern exposures to their personalities. They cannot get along well with their families, their people, or themselves. But at this point I am thinking that in this day any number of churches ought to be willing to face reality and wait for voices in their pulpits who do something other than ladle out some milk and water Pablum that happens to suit the taste of the idle crowd. Paul speaks of our religion becoming sounding brass and a tinkling cymbal, and it is easy for religion to land in that state when it is tied to a message that blathers and does not arouse. If the word of God is to be fire upon the earth, it must be spoken to people who think and who are willing to be disturbed. Something must lift people out of their earth-bound selves and set them free to become the larger selves they ought to be. There are great things to be said today, and blessed are the people who want to hear them.

Tertium Quid is an important character in Browning's *The Ring and the Book*. It is he who says:

> Nay, edge in an authoritative word
> Between this rabble's-brabble of dolts and fools.

That's exactly what I hope you will do as you preach. Get in a true word between the ambitious Ahabs and the false prophets who can kill the real spiritual development of a people and whose preaching does little but give a push toward the ultimate ruin of a nation and a world. The preacher who allows his preaching to be colored by nationalism may find himself riding the waves of popularity, but he will never acquaint his people with the demands of the kingdom of God. Bruce Catton in *This Hallowed Ground* tells us that when the slavery issue became so acute in Kansas, it was Henry Ward Beecher who said that a "Sharps rifle out there would have more moral persuasion than the Bible." It was Beecher and Charles

Sumner who helped sow the wind that eventually produced the whirlwind. Catton further observes that there was enough sowing of the wind down among the rabble without its being fanned from legislative halls and the pulpits of the land.

You in your pulpits today have something other to do than to tickle the hates, the prejudices, and the misunderstandings of your people. If, on the other hand, it is your desire to speak a sure word of prophecy to your congregation or to the club which you address, you may make some people unhappy with you. You may find yourself standing alone, and sometimes tears will blot the pages of your manuscript, and you will wonder whether it pays to have honesty and integrity of heart and mind. It is not what people want, but what they need of justice, mercy, and truth, that ought to be the burden of your preaching. It is standing in your place ringing the changes on Kingdom ideas rather than launching a campaign to your own personal advantage. Wouldn't you like to be a John Henry Jowett of whom a listener said one Sunday morning after hearing him preach in the Fifth Avenue Presbyterian Church, New York City, "What a terrible responsibility!"

I have wondered, too, all during my ministry how many people sitting in the pews of churches every Sunday morning are impatient with the preacher's interpretation of the gospel, and how many longing hearts inside and outside the church wait in vain for a word that speaks to their innermost souls, lifts the mists from their eyes, and opens

51

a way to which their whole being can respond. They may not be as articulate as was one of my daughters, when she wrote me one time, but it is of like essence. She wrote:

I've been meaning to write you this for some time now, but just haven't gotten organized to do so. I can hear you saying of course, "That's what I've been saying." As usual, however, I have to get there my own way and on my own understanding. I suspect that religion was justifiably horrified at the Darwinian proposition because the church could read the end of its superstitious hold over the minds of men in this new thing, science. We would better not sneer at the religion versus science heritage from the last century. The church had reason to quake. Here was a threat indeed to its position of unquestioned authority—of accumulated error.

If the church today is to have any influence on our time and place, it had better grasp its position of prophecy and leadership, and dismiss its superstitious practitioners, its witch doctors, its makers of terror—and face a tremulous new world. Let the veil of this old temple be rent again! Institutional Christianity has done little more than reconstruct the ancient temple with its ancient totems and taboos—but yet the Christian idea has gone abroad and worked its miracle upon men outside the temple.

If you are going to fulfill your prophecy and meet this modern mind, you will need some equipment. You will need to study. You have been to college and seminary, and I trust your mind has been set in the right direction. That is about all an institution of learning can do for any man. The years are ahead of you, and if preaching remains a fascinating business for you, it will be because your mind has been stimulated by study and because out of the pages of books and experience some golden truth has held you.

Now that the years have passed, I envy men of my age who had the privilege of sitting at the feet of some of the great intellects such as Josiah Royce, William James, Adolph Harnack, Rufus Jones, and a far greater galaxy than I am able to mention here. But I take comfort in the thought that these and other great minds have walked into my study through their books, and though I studied under men with lesser reputation, they kept step with the thinking of the day. I recall my church history professor saying with a bit of egotism, yet in modesty, concerning a great church historian, "I do not know as much church history as he, but I can teach it better." He probably could, for I never sat under a man who could teach with more clarity and who could make church history come alive better than he. One of the soundest bits of advice I ever heard escape his lips was what he said one day to our class: "If you young men will spend three or four hours a day in hard study, you will never reach a dead end." Somehow I wish that advice could pierce the armor of every young man as he sets out to preach today.

I do not know the caliber of the professors under whom you have sat, but there need be nothing to prevent you from choosing the masters of religion throughout the whole of your ministry. Toscanini once found a hurdy-gurdy man, half asleep, who was lazily droning through the "Toreador Song" from *Carmen*. Toscanini shook the startled player violently and commanded, "Faster, you fool! You play that as if it were a funeral dirge." The next day the hurdy-gurdy man had a new sign on his battered instrument. It read "Pupil of Toscanini." Hundreds of great masters in various fields of learning are saying to you, "Your preaching has no lilt to it, no wings of imagination, no good news, no story that quickens dead souls and lifts the burdens from heavy-laden hearts or spells victory in defeat." What is there to hinder you from becoming their pupils?

Not long since I was sitting in the company of a few younger preachers listening to another preacher talk about preaching. During the course of his remarks he said he understood that Ralph W. Sockman spends eighteen hours a week in the preparation of his sermons and that he consults any number of books. Later I overheard one of the young men ask, "How in the world can a man spend that much time on a sermon and do all the other things he has to do?" I thought I should like to have said to him, "That may not be the only reason why my friend Sockman has become an effective preacher and why so many people have waited on his radio preaching over a long stretch of years, but it is one of the reasons, and if ever you want to be a preacher of his caliber, you would better go and do likewise."

I know only too well that men are not created equal in mental ability or spiritual insight and that no matter how much one may apply himself, he will never reach the height of another. But I know also that preaching is not all genius or native ability. I heard S. Parkes Cadman say of another great preacher in New York, "I never knew a man who made such great use of so few talents as he." You may be sure that the great preachers of the past about whom you have learned in the seminary did not shake sermons out of their sleeves, nor do the great preachers of today spend the precious hours when they should be studying whittling sticks. It is as true now as when Elizabeth Barrett Browning wrote it that

> Earth's crammed with heaven,
> And every common bush afire with God;
> And only he who sees takes off his shoes;
> The rest sit round it and pluck blackberries.

When Edgar DeWitt Jones was writing his book *The Royalty of the Pulpit,* he wrote me asking if I would look up some material for him on a certain preacher about whom I happened to know a bit of history. He said, "Some of these men out of the past whom I am including in this volume were *near*-great preachers, and it is difficult to find material on them. I thought that since you had preached in Brooklyn where he once preached, you might know something about him." Fortunately in addition to the little I knew, I found considerable information about him in the Brooklyn papers of his day. It turned out that he was something more than a *near*-great preacher, though he had no far-flung reputation.

Perhaps it will be your fate to be even less than a near-great preacher. Your reputation will not spread beyond your own parish. Circumstances may never converge to the point of lifting you into the limelight. But your people will know, and God forbid that because of your intellectual laziness they will say, "Yes, he is a fine fellow and a good organizer, but a poor preacher." It is your business to be the best preacher you can become, regardless of whether or not it lifts you out of the place where you are now. It has been my good fortune to have some friends in the ministry who served small parishes all their lives, but who, when I came from hearing them preach, shone like bright stars in the firmament of my life. I recall some who, if set in some large metropolitan pulpit, would have equaled or surpassed many others whose names are writ large on the pages of newspapers. And I have known some prima donnas occupying pulpits of large churches who would do well to go and sit at the feet of some backwoods preacher.

If you will allow a personal reference, may I say that when I started out to preach, I deliberately chose to accept a call to a country parish of three small churches in the backwoods fourteen miles from a railroad. I am not telling you to go to the country, but I am sure it would be worth the while for many a young preacher, as it was for me, for the simple reason that a small rural parish offers time and opportunity for the preacher to develop habits of study. A young preacher in a busy urban church finds himself on committees, becoming involved in all sorts of extracurricular activities, and before he is aware of it, his energy is consumed in going places and doing things, and his busyness at 101 things leaves him little time to discipline his mind. He throws a few half-baked thoughts together on Saturday night, and on Sunday morning his people leave the church wondering why they had been there.

Below the village where I lived as a boy, a man owned a beautiful black, high-stepping race horse. Frequently I saw his trainer drive him through the village streets. I was fascinated with his magnificent action. Every time he took a step, his knee almost touched his head. Frequently he was entered in the county fair races, but he never won a race. One evening in the village store I heard a half-dozen farmers discussing the horse and why he could never win a race. After most of them had spoken their piece, one old farmer spoke up and said, "I'll tell you why he never wins a race: he can trot all day in a bushel basket." To that farmer it meant that the horse had beautiful action but no reach. And a successful runner, whether a horse or a man, must have reach to his stride. Somewhere I read that "life is judged not by its grasp, but by its reach; not by its failure to attain, but by its faith to dream and to dare."

Not a few ministers have plenty of action. They think they can save the world by attending many meetings, going to conferences, taking account of statistics, and playing the game of politics with the rest of the politicians in the church. The one thing needful—discipline of mind and heart—they forget.

As for me, I was cursed with two handicaps—a fear complex and I didn't know how to preach. As to the first, I was afraid of people, especially preachers who I thought knew more than I knew. In a discussion I was glued to my chair and my tongue froze in my mouth when I attempted to express an opinion.

I was elated one evening toward the close of my seminary career when my New Testament professor asked if I would accept a call to a church which had been organized in the seminary and where some college and seminary professors worshiped, but I shied away from it. I was afraid. Not for the world would I stand in that place. Had I known I had a fear complex, I might have known how to deal with it. It took me years to conquer this fear, and even today I sometimes find myself wrestling with it.

I also had to learn to preach. To be sure, I had a good course in homiletics. I had won some prizes in debating, oratory, and essay writing in college and the seminary. I knew something about the structure of a discourse and had on a number of occasions supplied vacant pulpits. But I didn't know how to preach. I didn't want to imitate anyone. I wanted to be myself, and throughout my ministry I have not been conscious of imitating any preacher, but I did want to sit awhile longer at the feet of the giants in the ministry. I wanted to know something of contemporary preaching. You may laugh, as many have laughed, at things emanating from Brooklyn; but I subscribed to the Monday edition of the *Brooklyn Eagle*. Every week it carried the sermons of some of the great preachers of that metropolitan area—Parkhurst and Merrill, both Presbyterians; Shaw, a Baptist; Melish, an Episcopalian; Goodell, a Methodist; Hillis, Cadman, and Boynton, all Congregationalists —the last named of whom I was destined to succeed twenty years later, although I did not dream of it then. I read their sermons, and no doubt some of their thinking crept into my own sermons.

I had a little library—three small shelves of books—and with a seven-hundred-dollar salary not much money with which to buy books. But the Carnegie Library in Pittsburgh, Pennsylvania, was not far away. I consulted a catalogue and found that the library would send me books if I paid the postage. Every month I sent for books, returned them, and got a fresh supply. Then one day the thought struck me that I might write a half-dozen prominent preachers and ask them if they would send me a list of a few books which they had found indispensable to their preaching. They sent the lists, and little by little as I had a few dollars, I added the books to my little library.

There through hard work and with infinite patience on the part of the farmer folk who came to my church, I learned a little about preaching. When I visited in their homes, they asked me questions and sometimes took good-natured issue with my sermons. All the people who were there nearly a half century ago have now gone, but my heart and mind still turn in the direction of the churches where I made a beginning at the business of preaching. I have never regretted going to that out-of-the-way parish.

As a student in the seminary I heard much of Sparhawk Jones. I never heard him preach, but his praises were being sung by all who knew and heard him. About the time he was closing his career in Baltimore, a young minister in his city set out to gain a reputation by parading sentimental news. People were filling his church, and one day on the street he was bragging of his success to Sparhawk Jones. Jones looked at him and said, "Yes, I have heard about you, and I hope your years will be crowned with success; but if you don't dig deeper into the well of spiritual resources and stop getting your sermons out of newspaper advertisements, you will soon find your pump sucking mud."

I do not know how any young preacher can be rescued from such a fate except by his own willingness to discipline his mind and heart. When I took that little rural parish, someone said to me, "Why are you going to bury yourself in the country?" I did not know what my future would be, the present was enough, and it did not occur to me that anything or anyone except myself could perform my obsequies. I knew only that I had to learn to preach and could not afford to become embroiled in a hundred activities which would leave no time except a few hours of a Saturday night to gather a few crumbs with which to feed a hungry flock the next day.

I had a desire, too, to have a liberal outlook on religion and a liberal attitude toward people and things. I have no hesitancy in saying to you young men that it takes liberal thinking to deal adequately with individual problems and with all the vexing problems of the social order. Only the liberal mind, whether in the pulpit or out of it, is *fit* to appraise the reasons why men and nations act as they do. For instance, don't make yourself ridiculous by falling back on the old dictum "Well, there are some things we must take on faith" when you are asked about the discrepancies, contradictions, myths and legends, in the Bible. Acquaint yourself with at least one authentic book on archaeology

60

such as *The Story of the Bible* by the German scholar Keller, bathe yourself in the sunlight of Fosdick's *The Modern Use of the Bible,* and along with your other translations and interpretations of scripture dig deeply into *The Dartmouth Bible* by Chamberlin and Feldman, and *Living Religions of the World* by Spiegelberg. You will be surprised, as I have often been, how hungry your people are for an interpretation of the Bible that makes sense and speaks to their intelligence. Paul was right when he said, "For God hath not given us the spirit of fear; but of power, and of love, and of a sound mind."

I could take up much space in telling what other books you should read, but I do not know that this would be helpful. Martin Luther put it in a nutshell when he said in his *Table-talk* that one should have some "sure and certain books" which you know as you know your best friends, books which should be "chewed and digested." Although you are no longer in the classroom and no professor will give you an examination, you will be before the tribunal of men and women in your own congregation who are sure to know more about some subjects than you know, such as the farmer, who knows his crops and his soil; and it will be wise for you to stick to the thing you know.

You ought, however, to be conversant with the march of present-day science. You ought to know the discoveries of the human mind. Obscurantism is a sin for the preacher. Even a little book on the nature of the green world and the starry heavens will at least open your mind to what is being discovered. Psychiatry and psychology too, plus spiritual healing, cannot be neglected by the preacher in a day when the human mind and soul are being explored as never before. To know character and conduct is an essential equipment of the preacher. Social needs and experiments, what constitutes good government, clean civic conditions, proper housing, how environment affects the growth or stultifying of character—all this ought to captivate the interest of the preacher. Acquaint yourself with historic movements, biography, and poetry. Last but not least, let theology be a guide but not your master. The last word on theology was not spoken by your professor in systematic theology. Theologies change, and they have made the divisions in the church wide and deep. But the love of God is eternal and his spirit unites, and only in Jesus is the Life and Light of men.

As a prophet of God who opens the gates of new life, remember that you are interpreting God to man, man to man, and man to himself. Your teacher in this respect need be no other than Jesus himself. I could never conceive of Jesus as spending all his time praying and reading nothing but the literature of his Hebrew fathers. He must have known the teachings of other men, and his mind must have roamed among the literature of other cultures. But he didn't consult erudite books for his illustrations. He found them in life about him. Strong men such as Nicodemus found an answer to their problems. So also did the common rank and file of men. They went home after hearing him, gathered their families about them, and said, "We have seen strange things to day." Others said, "We never saw it on this fashion." I imagine also that little children caught his message, because they sang their hosannas in the temple that day after he rode into Jerusalem.

It is not that you say something strange and new that will mark you as a prophet of God, but that you speak to the experience of youth and age, the college professor and the washerwoman. Bishop Francis J. McConnell said in a lecture on preaching that if someone says to you after you have preached, "I never thought of that before," the chances are he will never think of it again. But if he says, "Now you have made clear what I have been thinking about, but which was very hazy," you have preached an effective sermon. Someone asked the great premier of England William E. Gladstone what constitutes good public speaking. He replied, "The ability to send back in copious streams what the people send up to him in mist."

Give me the young, seeking mind in the church, or elsewhere, whether his life measures fifteen years or seventy, and you can have all the others whose minds stopped think-at thirty or thirty-five. We frequently hear it said that the great mass of people have ten-year-old minds. It seems so at times, but I find it difficult to believe, for Lincoln was always saying, "Trust the people; trust the people." If heads of governments and those who are set to guide the destiny of nations were as wise as he, the world would not be bathed in seas of blood. At any rate, Jesus said, "Except ye . . . become as little children, ye shall not enter into the kingdom of heaven."

As a young lad I sat Sunday after Sunday beside my mother in the village church. I wriggled just as any boy would wriggle, if not openly rebel, at being compelled to

63

sit under preaching he could not understand and in which God is a vague something sitting in the sky waiting to pounce on bad little boys and girls. But then when I was about nine, a new young preacher came to our church. I was to learn later that he was no simpleton, but finely educated and with a grasp of the elemental things of life. Which is rare indeed! I found my young mind taking in the preacher's words. He didn't talk down, but his thinking was clear and his words simple. I learned much about God and my relationship to him, and when I started to preach, I hoped I could think and speak as clearly as he. Any young preacher can do that if he loves people, thinks God's thoughts after him, sits where people sit, and preaches out of the overflow of his knowledge of the laws of God and the universe.

When Robert Norwood of St. Bartholomew's, New York, died at the age of fifty-eight, I determined to find out what made him a great preacher. I found two things. First, he was never afraid of truth no matter how disturbing it might be to him or to others. Second, instead of calling down fire on all the cults, he went about seeking the kernel of truth which was so persuasive in drawing to their fold so many people. He made the truth he found minister to his own preaching. If you find your people slipping away from your preaching you would better run quickly and examine yourself. It may be that you have got hold of the wrong end of the stick.

Finally, if world brotherhood, war and peace, are the two major problems of our day, they will become increasingly so during your ministry. If your preaching is to carry a note of prophecy, you can't spend all your time concentrating on personal purity and allowing the world to go as it will. During your seminary days the probability is that your professors—most of them—said little to you about meeting the problems in the spirit of nonviolence. Up to now our Western world has assumed the white man's superiority and that war is a valid way to settle public disputes, that Western sex mores, feelings, and ideas were everlastingly valid, that science is omnipotent, and that the state is divinely instituted. But unless your thinking is turned in another direction, you will not be serving your day and generation with any degree of wisdom and fortitude.

I won't argue with you about the fraudulency and futility of all past wars, nor tell you that there was no wisdom and fortitude on the part of our leaders in the American Revolution and the Civil War. We owe more than we can ever pay to the leaders who gave us the constitutional documents of the eighteenth century and to Lincoln for his Second Inaugural and the Gettysburg addresses. All I want to say is that these men had far less reason to be skeptical of political power than we have today. Further, the instruments of violence and coercion were mere playthings in those days compared with the weapons of today. Since that time we have had years of instruction in the social and psychological consequences of violence. Great and good men could then contemplate the use of military methods as a limited means to the attainment of a desired objective, which once realized would permit the re-establishment of rational procedures in resolving differ-

ences among men, parties, and nations. I doubt if great
and good men of the present can contemplate the use of
violence and coercion with the same optimism and equa-
nimity today. I doubt if they contemplate it at all.

You see the forces of evil in the world as clearly as I
see them, and when you ask me how they are to be sub-
dued and justice established, I have to answer that I do
not know; I have no answer beyond that employed by
Jesus. The familiar means of coping with evil have got
out of control—so far out of control that we no longer
dare to use them while we remain in our right minds. This
seems to me to be the common-sense interpretation of the
past forty years of history and a reasonable explanation of
the deep anxieties and confusion of present-day politics and
international relationships.

Regardless of how you view the person of Jesus, whether
as the second person in the Trinity or as a Man who ham-
mered out his character on the anvil of his own experience,
you can't get away from the fact that he saw the problem
of history and knew that the only way the world could
be saved was through suffering. If he lived in an ivory
tower, if his idea that man is capable of fellowship was
only a pipe dream and he was deluded in thinking that
war is against God's will, you will nevertheless have to
accept them and begin thinking in his terms if you want
to do something more than to lock him up in a creed and
a dogma. My soul, I don't see how you can go out into the
ministry, accepting along with all the other preachers the
one symbol of the church's faith and devotion, and then
in the midst of the most urgent problem of our times re-

ject it and explain it away. "Unto the Jews a stumbling-block, and unto the Greeks foolishness"—so Paul admitted when he called it the weakness and foolishness of God. If you don't preach that, what else is there to preach that comes anywhere near being the good news of God?

Within the space of the present generation only one man has offered a creative contribution to the problem of taking a hand in history. That man was Gandhi. He was the man of the hour for India, and he may be the man of the hour for the world. Another man, long before him and who has been regarded in some quarters as an atheist, wrote a sure word for all succeeding generations to look at. Tom Paine wrote: "An army of principles will penetrate where an army of soldiers cannot. It will succeed where diplomatic management would fail; neither the Rhine, the Channel, nor the ocean can avert its progress; it will march on the horizon of the world, and it will conquer."

Surely, young man, being a bearer of good news, you have an "army of principles" to proclaim. They are all embodied in the prophets, in Jesus, and in the saints of all ages. You may never be great in the eyes of the world, but there are great principles which can live in the treasury of your heart and mind, and the world will be better if you preach great principles and live by them.

I am not asking you to pose as a martyr and to act as though you had the final answer to all the problems of the world. The last thing Jesus wanted was martyrdom. But a more deadly thing than martyrdom is conformity. If ever a preacher lives in an ivory tower, it is when he lives in placid resignation to the world around him. To

keep out of this groove you will have to test the state of
your mind, explain your thinking to yourself before anyone will listen to you. But why bother all the time about
what other people think? Certainly you can't free yourself
from conformity by conforming to a program of either
the minority or the majority in which you can't quite believe.

At least the preacher of today and tomorrow who has
a scintilla of knowledge of the nature of God and the
essential principles of the Good News should be as honest
as the newspaper columnist who commented on the prayer
of a chaplain just before a nuclear blast was let loose in
Arizona. The chaplain prayed: "Unto us who are privi-
leged to draw aside the curtain into the secrets of thy universe, teach us that our whole duty is to love thee our God
and to keep thy commandments."

Presumably [said the columnist], there is at least one commandment that a chaplain is in no position to invoke. It would
seem a trifle awkward to enjoin "Thou shalt not kill" just before the detonation of a bomb with the power of several mil-
lion tons of TNT, capable of killing a few hundred thousand
of His children. Instead of the pious sonorities of this prayer,
I suggest a much more realistic invocation to be given by the
Representatives of the Lord whenever they happen to be
present on similar fraternal occasions. It would go something
like this:

*"Unto us who have the pride and the presumption to re-
lease the most devastating forces of nature, O Lord, be merciful. Protect us from cardiac confusion; preserve us from cere-
bral or coronary air embolism; guard us from the dreadful*

consequences of respiratory tract hemorrhages; allow us not to suffer from pulmonary edema; save us from the trauma of distended hollow viscera; withhold from us the horrors of hemorrhages in the central nervous system. Visit these catastrophes upon our enemies, not upon us, and we promise to love Thee and keep the commandments—all except one, O Lord."

This, at least, would be an honest and meaningful prayer. No nonsense, no hypocrisy, no solemn theological jargon to disguise and sanctify the purpose and the power of the bomb.

The Lord, I am sure, would not grant this prayer—but it would not, at any rate, be an insult to His intelligence and an affront to his benevolence. Sometimes I think He must be more discouraged by the blindness of his shepherds than by the folly of his sheep.[1]

When I was sitting one day at luncheon with the editor of a well-known magazine, we fell into conversation about religion, the church, and the preacher. Cynically he asked, "Are there any prophets in pulpits today?" Is that a commentary on the bankruptcy of the pulpit? God forbid! If it is, I could wish that a new generation of preachers, and then another, would arise to take the place of us who are rapidly going off the scene, and where we have failed, not only in the small areas of life, but in the larger, that they would see our error and commit themselves to larger views.

I hope when you stand in the pulpit, you will hear the political voices for what they are—a tinny, hurdy-gurdy sound. They belong to a lost youth, to the adolescence of

[1] Sydney J. Harris in the *Chicago Daily News*. Used by permission of General Features Corporation, 250 Park Avenue, New York City.

the modern power state, to the day of violence, and to the nonrational means of military force. It is not the realists who talk glibly of nuclear weapons and who are sophisticated in the mathematics of "calculated risk." The people who talk that way are the overgrown children living in the past. The realist of our time must be you, not because you have all the answers, but because you are aware of yourself at times and because, like Isaiah, you stand wondering at the Lord high and lifted up, and are like Jesus, who listened to and asked questions of the doctors and lawyers in the Temple, but who had to go back to Nazareth and work out a religion that would meet the problems of history.

THE PRIEST AT THE ALTAR

4

As a lad of about sixteen attending preparatory school, I spent a week end at the home of my roommate in a village not far distant. On Sunday morning I went with the family to the little white Methodist church at the top of the hill on the edge of the village and found myself seated beside an open window. It was a beautiful spring morning in May. Bees were humming, birds were singing, and through the window came the fragrance of lilac and honeysuckle.

It was a simple little church, such as dotted the landscape everywhere in my young days. There were no stained-glass windows, no altar, no cross, no candles, no cushioned pews—just a center pulpit, a chair for the minister, and a small communion table beneath the pulpit. I do not recall a choir nor the size of the congregation. At the appointed hour for the church worship to begin, the church bell rang, and a smallish gray-haired, neatly dressed minister, perhaps in his sixties, entered, took his place behind the pulpit, and bowed his head in prayer.

Simple as was the church, so the order of worship was simple—hymns, scripture, prayer, offering, sermon, and benediction. When the preacher arose to read the lesson, he read with a finely modulated voice, and he didn't stumble over the words. I do not remember what he read; I know only that I listened. Nor do I recall his prayer, except that I felt he was talking with God on my behalf. All I remember about the sermon is the text: "For, lo, the winter is past, the rain is over and gone; the flowers appear on the earth; the time of the singing of birds is come, and the voice of the turtle is heard in our land," taken from the Song of Solomon. Reflecting upon it since, I've always been glad that he didn't attempt to hook up that love song of the poet with the church.

Sunday was never a boresome day for me in my childhood. I went to church on Sunday as naturally and eagerly as I went to school on Monday. I roamed the hillsides in the afternoon, plucked the wild flowers, gathered the brown chestnuts in the autumn, and went to the maple-sugar camps in the early spring. Horace Bushnell's idea of Christian nurture must have somehow possessed the soul of my mother, for I was taught that religion is a natural and spontaneous experience, born in the soul, a gladsome thing to be nurtured through the years of sunshine and shadow, calm weather and foul, and to be laid down at last, not a perfect creation, but having developed a character which looks forward to an opportunity where

72

more of the dross may be purged from the personality under conditions more favorable than we can ever find here. If character building has any value at all, it has added significance if we believe that we are trying under God to create characters that are carried over into an eternal world.

But however valid this idea of Christian nurture which begins in the cradle, we must not discount those high moments which stab the human soul awake under the skillful and consecrated handling of an hour's church worship by the minister. It was so for me on that Sunday morning in that little plain church. When the last hymn had been sung and the benediction spoken, I went away feeling that this was the house of God and this the gateway to heaven. Many times since, I have driven by that little church with my family, and sometimes I have related my experience to my children in the hope that something as deep as that would light up their imagination and hold their souls in its grip. And as the years have passed, I have often thought that the preacher must have been a poet with poetry in his soul, else he never would have dared to preach on that text. It takes a heart overflowing with poetic justice and mercy that can make a church worship live in the soul of a young lad and light up his path to the end of his days.

How can it be that the years have not dimmed the recollection of that Sunday? Perhaps the text suited the mood of the spring morning. Certainly it was appropriate to the season. But I suspect it was something deeper. The preacher must have forgotten himself. If he lacked a formal education, he had not neglected the culture of his mind and heart. When he prayed, it was a pleading for the healing beams of God's love to shine into the hearts of the worshipers, and when he preached, he was speaking the language of the human soul.

Only the narrow-souled man speaks of a "right" and "wrong" type of worship, and only the ecclesiastical simpleton dogmatizes on this matter. I hold no brief either for a simple, free, and ornate worship and where no fixed order is either prescribed or compulsory, or for the elaborated, fixed, formal service, where prescribed forms and liturgical fashion prevail. The business of the preacher is to be an interpreter of the mind of Jesus as he understands it through reading the New Testament and to be loyal to the truth as he sees it. It ought to be a joy to know that others can worship God in other ways and perhaps in higher and better ways than you. Look again at Jesus, whom you regard as Lord and Master of your life, and learn his attitude of mind and spirit. When the disciples found a man who was not one of them, yet casting out demons in the name of Jesus, they wanted to call down fire on his head. But he said, "He that is not against us is for us." When the lepers were healed, he sent them back to their priests and their appropriate worship. He himself could praise God in the synagogue and the Temple, on the Mount of Olives or by the lakeside. Faith and love were primary; methods were secondary.

Not long since, I stopped at a church on the way to a preaching appointment of my own. It is a beautiful sanctuary that has all the appointments to catch the eye of the worshiper, lift his thoughts Godward, and set his soul on fire with truth, beauty, and goodness. The priest at the altar had all the advantages which the preacher in the little church on the hill did not have for making the worship hour a high adventure for the soul, an experience of spiritual exaltation, and in creating a desire to return next Sunday in eager anticipation for more—good choir, altar and reredos, cross, candles, beautiful symbolic lectern and pulpit, plus a stately liturgy. I have no quarrel with a liturgy, I was reared with one in my hand, and I become impatient with a sloppily conducted church worship service.

More than that, the preachers who think they can improve on the orderly arrangement of ritual which has come down through the ages must be an abomination to the Lord. I was talking with a devout Roman Catholic woman who told me that during the past Lenten season the Roman Catholics were instructed in the use of a new ritual which had been in preparation for twenty years. I am about as far removed from Roman Catholicism as a Protestant can be without repudiating the historic continuity of the church altogether, and I suspect much further than many preachers who think it their God-given prerogative to denounce in vitriolic language everything in the church that has built cathedrals of beauty, produced a Francis of Assisi, a Bernard of Clairvaux, a St. Cecilia, a Brother Lawrence with his *Practice of the Presence of God,* an Augustine with his *City of God,* and a Cardinal Newman with his "Lead, Kindly Light." But I have more respect for a church that takes twenty years to produce a ritual than for the Protestant ministers who assume to create a ritual of their own overnight. They would do better to stick to a simple form of worship rather than to use a conglomeration of meaningless, confusing words and phrases in their attempt to produce a more adequate ritual.

This preacher in this beautiful sanctuary used the established ritual of his denomination. It moved along with the rhythmic style intended. The congregation was well trained in its use, and participation in the worship was all that could be desired. What the total effect was upon the people as they left the church, I do not know; but as for me I had little sense of having worshiped God in the beauty of holiness. The preacher seemed to be giving a performance, and his artificial voice and sepulchral tones had nothing in them to make me see the Lord high and lifted up with his train filling the temple. Moreover, when he preached, he told me that my whole life was rotten. I resented that as much as Job resented the charge of his friends that all his troubles were the result of his sin. I like the rapier thrusts of the preacher that stab deep into my guilty conscience and make me cry with the publican, "God be merciful to me a sinner," but I also like to believe that the preacher will not be far from the mark in both his preaching and the conduct of the worship if he studies himself and his fellow men, understands the passions and longings of our common heritage, our desires and limitations and failures, the needs and sorrows of the world, and our links with the best and worst in life. Well may the preacher who seeks to lead his people in worship which William Ernest Hocking describes as the effort to "set God into the will to work there" make the prophet Micah's prayer his prayer:

Wherewith shall I come before the Lord, and bow myself before the high God? shall I come before him with burnt offerings, with calves of a year old? Will the Lord be pleased with thousands of rams, or with ten thousands of rivers of oil? shall I give my firstborn for my transgression, the fruit of my body for the sin of my soul? He hath shewed thee, O man, what is good; and what doth the Lord require of thee, but to do justly, and to love mercy, and to walk humbly with thy God?

God deliver us from the preacher who sets out to be "clever" in his conduct of a church worship! From the preacher, too, who deals in little things and forgets the great sentiments and truths that bind up and heal. He is a tragic sight in the midst of life's great agonies and sorrows. When I think of the burdened and puzzled I have seen—hearts that were covered by a twisted smile; businessmen who looked failure in the face for months; young men and women fighting back the rising passion of their red blood and being tempted to risk everything on some wild moment, only to have their prayers apparently unanswered; homes with a great big hole in them that nothing human could ever fill; nameless sorrows that tears can never ease and people who live on with nothing to live for; memories that are just one long ache and which bite like venom—when I think of these, I cannot help but think that many of the prayers peddled from altars and sermons driven with hammer blows into tender hearts are as thoughtlessly cruel as they are impertinent.

Let us have richness, color, and variety of worship. So long as men and women are different in build and outlook, they must be allowed to think differently and worship differently. However close together churches may move in the future, I hope you will not be among those who will seek to bring individuals and churches to a common level, for a common level is little more than a "dead level." A union of churches that spells uniformity and conformity would mean disaster to the church. We may well rejoice that we have come to the place where we build sanctuaries instead of auditoriums and where we are not afraid of symbolism. If God paints the sky in beautiful colors and man makes the desert to blossom as the rose, then there is nothing sacriligious about beautifying the house where men go to worship God. But this must not be a substitute for the presence of God in the inner life. If your priestly function is dependent upon the proper ecclesiastical arrangment of the sanctuary, you will succeed only in giving your church a form of Godliness which is in reality only a sepulcher of dry, lifeless bones. I somehow fear, when I see little souls ministering before altars and little minds and hearts standing in pulpits giving the people stones instead of bread, that the church has already come dangerously near to being only an organization rather than a life-giving organism. It will be a sorry day for the spiritual life of both you and your people if you allow the powers that be to intimidate you into slavishly following any order of worship against which the deepest and holiest instincts of your nature rebel.

Quite independent of differing methods and practices of worship is the spiritual quality of your people, the controlling ideas that bring them together, and how successfully the preacher can make God march through the hour's worship. When you prepare to enter the sanctuary, what is it that you want to do? Why are the people there? What is the first thing you would like to inspire in them? One of the distasteful things that catches my eye as I read the weekly bulletin of many churches is the constant urging of people by the preacher to come to church. If I were a layman and were urged week after week and in frequent pastoral letters to attend church, they would serve only to make me absent myself more frequently. You are the minister, and you wouldn't last long in any church if you were not there to act as ritualist and preacher. But the individual member is not under that compulsion. The thing that takes him to church every Sunday is something other than the thing that takes you to church. Perhaps your urging will bring him to church out of a sense of duty or because the day marks a special occasion, or maybe his church dues are languishing in the weekly offering envelopes, and it is time to pay up.

But one day something impels him to unite with the church. He waits on your ministry for a while. Then his attendance becomes intermittent. All the urging in the world will not fill his vacant pew at the worship service next Sunday, or the next, if he has lost the sense of gratitude and if you have failed to inspire in him a sense of wonder and awe. I know of nothing so devastating to the spiritual atmosphere of a worship service as the matter of taking things for granted. If the controlling element of astonishment at the goodness and mercy of God has gone from a people, the service degenerates into a formality, and your people will find more satisfaction on Sunday morning in engaging in other activities than in going to church.

I do not know how to tell you the method whereby you can inspire a sense of gratitude in your people except to say that it must first of all be part and parcel of your own inner life. I once asked a surgeon friend what makes a skillful surgeon. He quickly replied, "Good judgment. Any old plumber can make an incision in a patient's abdomen, and any old seamstress can sew it up; but what do you do when you find complications on the inside which you never saw before? No medical college can teach you that. It is something which belongs to the individual surgeon." So with the minister. Your college and seminary can instruct you in many details; your form of worship may have in it all that a true worship requires; but without knowledge of the human soul and of God on the part of the preacher, and no sympathetic understanding, your congregation will go away week after week without anything of wonder and awe, no gratitude, and nothing uplifting and cleansing.

"As the hart panteth after the water brooks, so panteth my soul after thee, O God," is the cry of the honest soul in your congregation as it waits for you to reveal unmistakably God in his righteousness as well as in his gracious pity. Whatever unworthy motivation may bring people to church, you must have confidence enough in them to believe that they are there to confess their faults. If that atmosphere does not prevail in your church, it may be that somewhere you have been remiss in bringing home to them that even an omnipotent God cannot forgive the heart that will not open to the pleading of God's love.

Then, too, the wonder and glory of any man's ministry lies in the fact that to you, a weak vessel, people look in a church service for your guidance and help amid the perplexities of life. Not being a strict ritualist and being inclined to a half-free and half-liturgical service, more frequently than otherwise I have fashioned prayers out of the depth of my own and the people's need. If you do that, you will be amazed times without number how someone will speak to you at the close of the service, call you on the telephone, or write you a note, saying, "Won't you please let me have the prayer? I have a special need for it." Personally I covet that kind of interest more than the effusive praise of a sermon. It bespeaks love for and trust in the minister. People live in a tangled web of things; difficult problems confront them every day; what their duty is in a given situation, they hardly know; their pathways diverge, and they do not know the way to take. The preacher who knows how to pray as well as how to preach will soon find this man with an ethical problem on his hands, this woman with a family situation, this young man and woman with the decisions of life confronting them, seeking out the preacher for his help and guidance. It is more than enough to make him cry, "Who is sufficient for these things?" Think of it—people looking to you to point the way! Troubled souls looking to you for a sure word to show them the path Jesus trod and to assure them that no one gets lost when he walks the right road.

Moreover, this service which you will conduct next Sunday must say something about obedience. Not long since, a minister of thirty years spoke his discouragement to me about the discrepancy between people's beliefs and their actions. What could be done about it? Was there ever a minister who did not find this paradox? "What I would, that do I not; but what I hate, that do I," is as true now as it was with Paul. It is not as easy for people to do the will of God as preachers sometimes think it is. People are doing battle in situations which never touch you. Even if they do touch you, people are not surrounded with the restraining influences which are yours. But any worship service that has no strong emphasis on obedience is value-less. It may be beautiful and deeply emotional, but worship is more than praise, it is *life;* and your service on Sunday will be a failure if it does not strengthen the spirit of obedience and moral resolve.

Let us not condemn the dramatic in a church service. I have often wished I had more of it in my make-up. Not shownmanship, not antics, which call attention to the ritualist, but the ability to set in contrast the difference between good and evil, light and darkness, humility and arrogance, love and hate, forgiveness and revenge, and all the qualities of a Godlike character as over against selfish aspiration that produces little rather than large-hearted souls in a church. Jesus was a natural dramatist. He could

82

say more in a story than in a sermon. He could teach forgiveness better by washing the feet of Judas than by giving a definition of forgiveness, and he could tell the world more about his kingship by riding into the city of Jerusalem on a donkey than by talking about it.

What I do deplore and what you may well avoid is the play for emotionalism. What a lovely service! What a sweet sermon! What beautiful flowers! I could hardly keep the tears away all through the service! These are the emotional outbursts which the preacher hears, and they are often music to his ears. But a little of this ought to be enough to send him back to the vestry in scalding tears. For what is the value of a worship hour if emotions are not translated into life and action? An emotion that does not cleanse, that does not transform character and conduct, is worse than none—it is a moral danger. Every emotion felt and rejected leaves the worshiper a worse man. Making a play for shoddy emotionalism will leave the souls of the congregation harder than before, and in the end the preacher will be little more than a charlatan.

Maybe by one contrivance or another you will fill the pews at every church service, but if that is the end-all and be-all of your ministry, you would stand more upright in the sight of God if you would employ your talents in some commercial enterprise. But the kingdom of God is at stake waiting for the preacher to state its principles and demands, and if the worship in the sanctuary leads to no purer lives and no concerted action in behalf of the world's woes, then your ministry is a failure. Worship is not an end in itself. The church is not the kingdom of

83

God. It is a goodly fellowship of souls on its knees praying in a manner that will set it standing on its feet saying, "This is the way, walk ye in it."

"I was glad when they said unto me, Let us go into the house of the Lord." This was the peculiar gift which Jesus wanted to leave with the world. The world was a slaughterhouse then, and it is a slaughterhouse now. In the upper room he could hear the tramp, tramp, of marching soldiers. He could hear the men down in the courtyard nailing his cross together. But in the midst of it all he said, "Be of good cheer; I have overcome the world." That's the joy the preacher and his people should carry into every church worship service. Why be so solemn? Why should our worship be mournful and plaintive, our music so sad, our prayers so lugubrious, and our emphasis so much upon sin and so little upon grace? When the prodigal son returned from the far country, the father did not call a solemn prayer meeting. He provided music and dancing, and he told the complaining elder brother, "It was meet that we should make merry, and be glad: for this thy brother was dead, and is alive again; and was lost, and is found."

I have rarely interfered with the choir. It is the war department. But I recall saying to one choir leader that I hoped the choir would never again sing the anthem that has the words "Oh that I had wings like a dove! for then would I fly away, and be at rest." My people did not need that prayer. They had been resting long enough. And I didn't need it. I had felt often enough the disposition to give up in despair. I needed more the exortation to

84

Ezekiel, "Son of man, stand upon thy feet." I tell you young preachers, and you older ones, that it is a grave misreading of Christianity to call it, in the language of Carlyle, the "creed of sorrow," and it is a morbid outlook on the life of Jesus to be forever calling him "a man of sorrows, and acquainted with grief." I do not need to be told that his way was often strewn with heartbreaks, but I know, too, that he could see the humor as well as the pathos of life, that he rejoiced at a banquet, and that the living of life itself brought its joy and satisfaction. Victory was in his life and teaching, and his way spells the ultimate redemption of mankind in a redeemed world. Why linger before the stations of the cross and forget the glory in his heart as he trod the way to Calvary? Why come to church with sober faces and depart with depressed spirits? Certainly there is a sense of propriety that belongs to church-going that is different from that which prevails at a baseball game. But what a dull business church worship can be! Little wonder that youth looks at religion as something that robs life of all joy rather than enriches it!

Some time ago I read—I do not remember where—that three things characterized the early Christians—they were always courageous, always cheerful, and always getting into trouble. What has robbed the church of these characteristics? Surely many of our churches can lay little claim to any great amount of courage in the face of the fear which politicians and militarists have thrown about the minister and the church. Both preacher and church can so easily sink to the level of radio and television propaganda. Cheerfulness, too, has taken its departure in the face of the unhappy peace in the world. As to getting into trouble, the scare of subversion and treason has been so effectively drawn that even the church moves along the line of the least resistance to anything that seems revolutionary after the manner of its Lord and Master. Joy! The early church impressed the world by its note of supremacy in Jesus and that it could face the morrow in the assurance of God.

It is not necessary that we shout our joy from the housetops, or go about proclaiming how courageous we are, or rush into trouble for the sake of martyrdom. There are a joy and a confidence that are quiet and serene, and as lovely as a summer's day. We don't need to forget the sufferings of the world, indeed our love for humanity will make us regard the sufferings of others with outstretched hands of mercy and kindness, but we can also look through them to see the dawn of a better day.

In relating my experience in the little church in the long-ago, I said that the preacher did not stumble over the words as he read the scripture. It is on this note that I should like to bring the function of the priest at the altar to a close. I could wish that this part of the worship of God would be more adequately and reverently handled than is true with a large number of preachers. Many of us older preachers remember the utmost satisfaction we experienced when we heard Charles R. Brown of Yale Divinity School quote the scripture from memory. Quoting from memory came as natural to him as breathing because it had been a lifelong exercise begun in childhood and continued through a long stretch of years. Doubtless

86

there are other preachers who are equally well practiced in this direction, and all of us would be happy if we could read from memory even a much smaller portion of the Bible. But the preachers I have heard assaying to read the lesson in this manner have made a pretty poor fist of it. To copy or to ape another's ability without having entered into the other man's experience can serve only to make one ridiculous and to make the worshipers feel that the preacher is doing a bit of showing off.

It is not necessary that the preacher quote the lesson from memory any more than it is necessary to preach without a manuscript, but it is essential that he be familiar with what he *does* read. Unfamiliarity not only conveys the impression that the passages have been chosen hastily and carelessly a few minutes before the service, but the casual and all too frequently unintelligent reading tells the truth about the little value the preacher puts upon the reading of the scripture. It argues mightily against the preacher's true duty and function. In any case, the preacher thinks that the scripture reading is an easy thing, whereas it is the most difficult thing in the service if it is to be done well. I have more than once or twice felt and have occasionally told my congregation that if I could just adequately read the great text I had chosen for my sermon, so that its real impact would strike home to their innermost being, I would dismiss them without a sermon, for nothing I could say would remain with them as well as the passage itself. I recall, in reading the biography of John Henry Jowett, that one Sunday morning while he was reading the story of the cleansing of Naaman by

Elisha the prophet and came to the words "And his flesh came again like unto the flesh of a little child," he read it so vividly, so captivatingly, that the people felt they were seeing the miracle performed before their very eyes.

Perhaps you will never reach that height of perfection in reading the scripture lesson, but there is no excuse for lightly regarding the place of the scripture reading in the sanctuary. If you have never learned to read well, go quickly and learn now. Choose your passages carefully and study them. Read them over time and again in the privacy of your study. No man can read well or be able to convey the meaning of what he reads to others if the meaning is not clear to him. The secret of good reading is to get at the heart of the passage, live in its atmosphere, so that you not only know the meaning but *feel* it. If you will do this, you will know how to read the different types of lessons. If it is narrative, read it as such; if dramatic, may you have eyes to see and heart to feel the situation, and read it dramatically but reverently. And poetry—Who can read it well? There is much of it in the Bible to be read, and although you may not be a poet yourself, if you have a poet's soul, something will catch fire so that those who listen will know that God's love is burning brightly on the altar of your heart. In the end, in all your scripture reading forget what you have learned of oratory and elocution. Be natural in your speech, articulate, and read as though you were delivering God's message to famished men. And please, oh, please, avoid making comments. Good reading is its own commentary and outdoes anything you can say. If I were in church and the preacher should begin to comment on the passage he was reading, I would be tempted to shout, "Let it stand on its own feet and don't spoil it." I have little sympathy for the preacher who stops in the middle of a passage to explain. Good reading will explain as much as is necessary at this point in the service. It is better than anything you can say about it.

Then, too, avoid the beaten track. There is more to read in a Sunday service than the great passages from Isaiah, the fifteenth chapter of Luke, the twelfth chapter of Romans, or the thirteenth chapter of First Corinthians. There is more, too, to be read in the more highly liturgical churches such as the Episcopal and Lutheran than the appointed Gospel and Epistle lessons for the day. Any number of people in your congregation are not great Bible readers, but I have never heard any complaint or opposition to the reading of noble scripture passages either in the home or in church when read by one who can read well. In fact, people like to hear them read, and with a full selection and careful preparation you can make scripture reading a delight and an education for your people.

What details I have left out were omitted deliberately. Principles of worship are your chief concern, and if you are a wise master of the art of worship, you will know in your own conscience the details that may serve to make the hour in church a lasting experience for the worshiper, not merely stirring his emotions but compelling him to action.

Whatever form of worship you may use, never forget that you can be the kind of saint described by someone as a "person through whom the light shines." God waits for the light to shine through you to the people in every church service you conduct.

MANKIND IS YOUR BUSINESS

5

WILL YOU BE SURPRISED IF I TELL YOU I LIKE THE WORD "evangel" but am not so fond of the word "evangelistic"? Both words stem from the same root, but "evangel" retains its pristine beauty—the good news of God—while "evangelistic" has fallen from its high estate. "Evangelistic" smacks so much of high-pressure salesmanship, stage setting, hustling committees, a highly trained and efficiently conditioned organization—all for the purpose of focusing attention on the evangelist; and it doesn't make much difference who the evangelist is, just so he talks about God and salvation in a way that hypnotizes people into believing that he has been taken into the secret counsels of God and knows the last word about religion.

It has likewise fallen into bad company with the ecclesiastical promotional committees. Literature of a various sort rolls off the presses in ever-increasing volume and out to the minister's study. "This is the year," it tells the minister, "for the greatest advance in membership in the history of the church. Organize your laymen for a great drive. Get behind the Great Crusade. More people than ever are looking toward the church. Put on a great church-going campaign. Invite the stranger and have a hand-shaking committee in the narthex of the church every Sunday morning. Get the visitor to sign on the dotted line. The church must let the world know that it is alive. If everybody pitches in, the year's statistics will show the largest gain ever, more money will have rolled in to build more churches, and the missionary cause will be advanced. We will all have a jolly good time together, and when the last nose has been counted, we will praise God with grateful hearts, 'for the Lord God omnipotent reigneth.' "

Evangelism! It works! The church is a success! While Jesus still hangs on his cross and weeps, Paul still sits in his dungeon waiting for the great hosts of the church to join him, and the little band of followers of the first century are still wondering when this Roman holiday will be over.

You, young men, will be caught in this wave of evangelism. You are young, eager, enthusiastic. You are part of the church. You don't want to appear queer or reactionary. You don't want to be an obstructionist. The church has work to do, and you have been called into its ministry. You want to speak a good word for Jesus Christ and do the work that has been committed to your care. Your hopes are high and your heart leaps for joy as you take your place among those who laid their hands on your head a little while ago.

I hope the years will always find you in pursuit of your deepest and most precious desires. And you will if you bear about with you the good news of God, if you are overwhelmed with the love of Jesus, if you understand that the way to the kingdom of heaven is through the narrow gate of the human heart, and if the supremacy of Jesus is exalted above opinions, conclusions, and practices. Timeservers, go-getters, and opportunists, successful as they may seem to be, are sickly pale alongside the preacher who would be an evangel.

I shall never forget the joy I experienced when I learned for the first time that "evangel" means the "good news of God." I recall, too, what it meant for me to feel that when I went out, I was going to be the bearer of good tidings. One thing, however, I didn't know and don't know yet—how vast the good news is and what a wide range of territory it covers—but I am sure it is the last word of God to man, and we can't know its full effect until not only the preacher but the people recognize that they are in possession of something which is for the healing of the nations.

However, for long years I have been wondering how to *be* an evangel. And if you are honest with yourself and wiser than I was, you will sit down now and ask, Just how do I become a bearer of good tidings? You will meet more people in the course of your lifetime than you will see of a Sunday, even on Easter, in church. You will be in your pulpit a possible fifty-two hours a year, and with a minimum of a month's vacation only forty-eight hours. Part of every day will be occupied in sermon preparation. Some hours during the week you may find yourself reading books, magazines, and newspapers. If you are a busy preacher, your sleeping hours will not be long. Much of your working time during the 365 days in the year will be spent with people. Your evangel cannot be kept in the pulpit waiting to be continued next Sunday. You will carry it with you, and its worth will depend not so much upon what you say as upon what you are and do.

In short, the good news will be you. People will forget much of what you say, but they will not forget you. Booker T. Washington, telling of the influence which shaped his life, said:

For a year and a half I lived working for Mrs. Ruffner. What I learned from her! It was like breathing new air. I could never say in words what she taught me, for it was not taught in words but in life. She never pronounced such abstract expressions as "frankness" and "honesty"—they radiated from her, like sunlight streaming silently through a clean window, as she spoke of the tasks she set me. I have repeated ever so many times the story of what Mrs. Ruffner taught me by the way she lived in her home—lessons as of great a value to me as any education I ever had in all my life.[1]

It all turns around this—How much do you love people, not for what they can do for you by way of making you a success, but just because they are people? A woman

[1] From "The Washed Window" in *A Harvest of Stories* by Dorothy Canfield. Used by permission of Harcourt, Brace & Co.

who lived in China for forty years and whose friendship
I have prized for a long time told me of a young missionary
who came to China just about the time the bandit raids
had stopped. One day he went to see a Chinese woman
who had lost her husband and children at the hands of
the bandits.

"What did you say to the woman?" my friend asked after
he returned.

"I told her," he replied, "that it was the will of God
and that she should submit to the will of God."

"What do you know about the depth of sorrow in that
woman's heart?" she asked. "What kind of God are you
bringing to China? I should think you would bring a
sorrowing God, a God who is distressed over the sufferings
of his children, a God who grieves because hardhearted
and hard-fisted men can make countless Rachels weep
for their husbands and children, who are not. Let me
suggest that you forget the God you were taught about by
your minister and your theological professors, and show a
God of mercy and compassion by living a life of mercy
and compassion. Stop talking about submitting to the
will of God to a woman who has lost her entire family.
Just go about, as Jesus did, binding up wounds and letting
your light shine into the dark corners of people's lives.
Perhaps there is a menial task you can perform, tears
that can be dried by a kind deed, and love for God that
can be kindled in many hearts because of your love for
them."

It changed the young man's concept of the whole missionary enterprise. Would that some such concept of God

could grip the heart and mind of every young man as the seminary doors close behind him and before he essays to become an evangel. William O. Douglas of the United States Supreme Court tells a moving story in his book *An Almanac of Liberty*. A Christian missionary went from England to India to save the heathen from their blindness and bring them into the light. One day in the streets of a crowded city he saw a beggar seated on the pavement, his body covered with sores. He felt moved by the man's misery and went to speak to him. He told him that he had brought him a truth that could save him—the truth of salvation through Christ. The beggar listened for a long time. Finally he said, "You have spoken much of believing. Did your Christ say anything about how men should live?"

"Yes," said the missionary, "he said that we should love one another, that we should love our neighbor as ourselves."

"So did all the great teachers," replied the beggar, "but which of their disciples acts upon it? You yourself—do you do what your Christ commands?"

"I try to," replied the missionary.

"Good!" said the beggar. "Then bring a bowl of water and wash my sores."

The missionary felt a little sick. He said he would come again when he had more time. Which he never did. But wherever he went, the words went with him: "You yourself—do you do what your Christ commands?" "I try to." "Good! Then bring a bowl of water and wash my sores."

That is what the whole world is asking—especially its

destitute and forlorn, who live in desolate places. Do you believe your religion? Do you do what it commands? Then cleanse the world's sores, bind up its wounds, and heal its miseries. What if this should become the purpose of the church and the preacher?

Thomas Beecher was not as famous as his brother, Henry Ward Beecher, but his biographers tell us that in some respects he was a greater preacher. When he went to Elmira, New York, he said to his people one Sunday morning: "I don't intend to do any casual visiting among you. But this I will do and want to do—if there is anything I can do for you, I will gladly do it. I will sit by your sick, I'll listen to your troubles, take you where you want to go if you have no conveyance, run errands if you have no one else to run them for you. I'll even cut your wood for you." They took him at his word, for he meant it. Thereafter during the whole of his ministry in Elmira it was not unusual to see Thomas Beecher trudging along the street with saw and sawbuck on his shoulder, going to cut some family's wood.

Sounds strange, and humorous too, doesn't it, in this day of automatic gas and oil burners? But one could wish that the spirit of it could be caught by the young men and women who have heard of the Son of man who came not to be ministered unto but to minister. It takes time and love and a heart wide open to the crying needs of a parish to do the work of a ministering evangel. It can't be done in a five-minute interview in your study or in ringing twenty doorbells in an afternoon and then gleefully reporting to your official board that you made two hundred calls last

97

month. You don't get nervous breakdowns by laying your-self under the needs and burdens of your people. You get them because you are frustrated at not being noticed as much as you think you ought to be, by being disappointed at not receiving that call to the church with the prestige, by allowing your work to get on top of you instead of keeping on top of your work.

It will be a great day in your life, although you may not know it until years after, if ever a lad or a lass, a young man or woman, a few persons, a dozen of them, or maybe fifty; some skeptic, someone who finds it hard to believe in God; some storm-tossed soul out of whose life has gone all the music; some man or woman groping, searching, for a religion that satisfies both mind and heart, discover their own inner sanctuary just because out of your heart and in your countenance there has shone the light of the kind of God that satisfies the deepest instincts of the human soul. Never mind the time it takes. Jesus spent a dinner hour with Zacchaeus, and a new world of values flooded the soul of the tax collector. He sat a long while on the coping of the well in Samaria talking with a woman, answering her questions, dispelling her outworn conception of religion, and showing her a universal God who could fill the heart's sanctuary of both Jew and Samaritan.

As I entered the chancel on the first day of a week's noonday Lenten preaching in a downtown church in Detroit, my eye fell on a little plaque with a saying inscribed on it, not by a Christian, but by the Hindu poet and philosopher Tagore. It read: "When you took your leave, I found God's footprints on my floor." *"You took your leave"*—from where? From the home where you just now called; from the street corner where you talked with a man or woman; from the bank where you had dealings with the teller, the store where you made a purchase, the elevator where you rode with a Negro operator, the card table where you sat and played with three other people—strangers perhaps—who will never come to hear you preach. They are like ships passing in the night, only to go on and never to be seen again. What kind of footprints do you leave? Footprints of forbidding ecclesiasticism? Of arrogance? Of controversy? Or footprints of love, courtesy, humility, and radiant personality? You don't live your life in a vacuum. You make religion either an absurdity from which people will turn away or the compulsive power of a new affection.

In the early days of the Massachusetts Bay Colony there was a colony of lepers on the mainland. Only one doctor, a Dr. Parker, would minister to their needs. Soon his practice fell off. Folks were afraid he would transmit the leprosy to them. So one after another of his patients deserted him. Then the lepers were moved to an island in Buzzard's Bay. But Dr. Parker continued to visit them.

Came a day when a Portuguese sailor lay dying. He was a Catholic and asked for a priest to give him the last rites of the church. A priest was sent for and rowed over to the island to grant the man absolution. The priest sat by the bedside of the Portuguese sailor and questioned him about his devotion to the church. Then he asked, "Do you believe in God?" The sailor lifted his emaciated form on his elbow, looked the priest in the eye, and replied, "I do not know. I do not know if I believe in God or not. But I do believe in Dr. Parker."

If I could start my ministry again alongside of you and could reach out over forty-seven years to the place where I am now, I think I would ask myself, "How many people will see God in me, or as Tolstoi said of Abraham Lincoln, a 'Christ in miniature'?" and I wouldn't care whether they could give a definition of God or not, or write a creedal statement, or pass a successful examination on a long list of churchly doctrines. Whatever you may hold about the church, it does not seem to have entered into the hope of Jesus for the world. He did not organize a ministry. He did not think in terms of a hierarchy or a church. He did not ordain sacraments. These things came later, and it was inevitable that they should come. When people are of a certain mind and heart, they get together in groups for a common cause. Little or nothing can be done with ecstasies until we organize them. But that does not mean that the ecstasy itself postulates any specific organization. Jesus brought an ecstasy about God into the world, leaving it to his followers to organize.

For example, you may believe that the whole of Christianity is contained in the sacrament of the Lord's Supper. Indeed, as I look back over my life, one of the never-to-be-forgotten days in my experience was my confirmation day at the age of twelve, when I took my first Communion and joined in singing the hymn "Jesus, I My Cross Have Taken." And somehow down through the years every time I have handed the elements to the officers, I have found myself saying inwardly, "This is the judgment of the world." And frequently, too, a little incident in a Scottish kirk would come to mind. A young girl with a sin upon her soul wandered into a Communion service one Sunday. She was weeping and as the elements were being passed, thought she was unworthy and was about to refuse them. An old elder, seeing her tears, nudged her elbow and whispered, "Take it lassie; it's for you." And she took it.

Any number of folks find comfort in this sacrament and go from it with a new song in their souls. But what I should like to convey to the young minister is this: Don't allow any ecclesiastical arrangement to prevent you from being charitable in your judgment of any man who finds it hard to comply with some of the things you may regard as essential. Some will never hold your belief, and some will find it hard to believe at all. When I went to Brooklyn, I found an old man who said to me, "I will always come to church except on Communion Sunday."

"Why not on Communion Sunday?" I asked.

"Because I don't believe in it," he replied. So he never came on Communion Sunday. But when I officiated at his funeral a few years later, the church was crowded with folks who loved him. Two Jews and their two sons with tears streaming down their cheeks asked, "May we go to the cemetery?" I replied that the interment was private but was sure the family would not object. They clasped their hands in mine and said, "Oh, thank you, we will go. He was an honest man. He was good to us." Sure enough, when we lowered the body, the four Jews were there

101

weeping for the man who was honest and who was good to them.

When John P. Altgeld, whom Vachel Lindsay, the poet, called the "Eagle That Is Forgotten," was an old man broken on the cross of bigotry for having pardoned the Haymarket "bombers" a few decades ago in Chicago, Clarence Darrow, the noted criminal lawyer and proclaimed atheist, who had run for and won election to the Illinois Legislature at Altgeld's request, took Altgeld into his law firm. At Altgeld's funeral Darrow said, "In the great flood of human life that is spawned upon the earth, it is not often that a man is born. The friend and comrade that we mourn today was formed of that infinitely rare mixture that now and then at long, long intervals combine to make a man."

Better guard your judgment, my dear young preacher, all through your ministry, lest the man you judge so harshly and who does not conform to your churchly beliefs turns out to be a better man than you. I imagine Judas, after he kissed his Lord in the garden, remembered, not so much the supper in the upper room, but the splashing of the water in the basin at the hand of the Man who stooped there and forgave the darkness of his mind. How many times in my ministry have I wished that people who considered it a sin to absent themselves from the Communion would look again at the picture of the heartbroken Jesus washing the feet of the man who helped to break it! A humble Jesus teaching me forgiveness of my worst enemy from that upper room is more significant than the observance of the Lord's Supper.

102

Don't sneer at the words "a good man" as though there was something lacking of Christian thought and philosophy in his make-up. How would you like to have an entire congregation of men and women who were good after the manner in which Jesus defined goodness? People as generous as the atheistic Darrow? People who were kind and loving toward all racial groups as was the old man who would not attend Communion? People who were as humble as the publican praying, "God be merciful to me a sinner"? Jesus talked about people who loved the chief seats in the synagogue and those who chose the best seats at a feast. But when he really wanted to define goodness, he dramatized it that night when he stooped and washed the disciples' feet. "Know you what I have done? If I then, your Lord and Master, have washed your feet; ye also ought to wash one another's feet."

What Jesus called pride, our modern psychology books call a superiority complex. And if you have never come to the place where you have dealings with that small but ubiquitous section of your church who feel superior to the rest of the congregation, not because of their worth but because they are tagged "Special, Handle with Care," you will know why it was said of Jesus, "The common people heard him gladly."

David Seabury in his book *How Jesus Heals Our Minds Today* describes a preacher by the name of Fredric Huntington Marlborough who was proud of the fact that he had seven generations of preachers behind him. He did not like to remember when he was a brat of eight or nine years, how his hair was always tousled, his nails dirty, and his speech full of profanity. He was proud of his present speech and that like all Marlboroughs before him he had a beautiful church. He was perfectly upright, well groomed, and his sermons tasteless, a matter which did not give many of his parishioners much concern. In short, he was a perfect Pharisee. But fate was not so unkind as to spare the Rev. Huntington Marlborough from regeneration. He was saved, but not until thirty years later.

He started off on a journey which he expected would carry him round the world. But when the ship put in at the South Sea Islands, he thought he would stay on and see the missionary work which his church was doing. Awhile later he took a small steamer to a neighboring island, but when the ship landed, he was not aboard. No one knew what had become of him, but it developed that he had fallen overboard and been rescued by a little black fisherman.

For the next eighteen months on the island to which his rescuer took him he lived a life such as he had never lived before. There were few white persons, mostly savages, and instead of his teaching them, they taught him. He received important lessons in communal eating, sleeping, and bathing. He began to dream, to see life in retrospect, and to become a child again.

At length he was rescued, had a breakdown on the ship, and eventually found himself in a hospital in San Francisco. There he went through all the rigors of a deep analysis. By the time he was finished, he saw how drab his life had been, and in the end the last shred of arrogance and pride had disappeared. He became a human being, aware of his limitations as well as of his gifts, which after all is an essential step in becoming a son of God.

It was to change men's minds from arrogance and pride to humility before God and man that Jesus probed so deeply with his message "Thou shalt love the Lord thy God with all thy heart, and with all thy soul, and with all thy mind, and with all thy strength: this is the first commandment. And the second is like, namely this, Thou shalt love thy neighbour as thyself. There is none other commandment greater than these."

A good man also according to Jesus identifies himself with humanity everywhere. Wouldn't you love to preach to a church full of people who are bent on doing just that? When Christianity became a spontaneous religion and took upon itself the authority to cut clear across boundaries and dared to speak about Jesus Christ outside the confines of Jerusalem, it was a man named Barnabas, "a good man, and full of the Holy Ghost," who was there to champion the cause. Jesus had done this when he met a Sidonian woman whose daughter was ill and when the Samaritan woman came out from her village to draw water at the well of Jacob.

The good news would never have reached beyond Jerusalem had it not been for the lessons such as these which he taught the disciples. It was hard to learn the lessons, and one of the best of them, Peter, had to learn them later when he was told in a vision to call nothing unclean. Strange, isn't it, that we know so little about the men who companied with Jesus? I have been forced to wonder many times during my ministry what would have become of the good news had it been left for them to declare. It was Paul who never saw Jesus in the flesh, who caught his spirit, his fire, and his enthusiasm, and who found himself telling Peter to his face that he had caught precious little of his Master's teaching.

Kipling said, "If all men count with you. . . . If you can . . . walk with Kings—nor lose the common touch, . . . you'll be a Man." [2] If all men count! If your people are going to learn that, they may have to learn it from you. The self-conscious feeling of national, religious, and racial groups that they are the people who count is the fountainhead of the world's flood of woe.

Bigotry, which you will find in your church, was not spawned in Germany or any other particular place. It has been expressed by people everywhere, and alas, by Anglo-Saxons. Here, for instance, was Lady Astor, stepping off the ship that brought her to America and saying to reporters: "Look at Russia, Germany, Italy, Spain—and France is nothing to write home about. Those people have never read the Bible as we have in the Anglo-Saxon countries. It is that which forms the character of the Anglo-Saxon people and their way of thinking." Here in our American culture and in our churches we seem to have taken a page out of Lady Astor's book. As Halford E. Luccock says, "Volumes could easily be compiled, giving the American version of Hebrews 1:1 'God having of old time spoken with the fathers in the prophets by divers portions, hath at the end of these days spoken in the marvellous achievements of the American people!' "

[2] From "If." Used by permission of Doubleday & Co. and A. P. Watt & Son.

I read, not long since, of a suburban woman's club that invited Countee Cullen to come and read poems. But the club finally canceled the engagement because it was suddenly discovered that it was the custom to serve tea after the program, and that could not be done with Countee Cullen present. Some wag commented on it in parody:

> Poems are made by fools like me,
> But only God can come to tea.

And when the Georgia Legislature determined to prohibit interracial sports and to impeach six members of the United States Supreme Court for ruling against segregation, B. Jo Kinnick from California sent the "Black Boy's Question" to the *Saturday Review:*

> When I check out my robe and harp
> And turn in death's pale shroud,
> Which way in Heaven should I turn
> To find the Jim Crow cloud? [3]

Do you object to having men and women in your church who are good enough to stand above racial bigotry? Jesus would hardly call a church or a church member good whose factional practice of Christianity would lead only to the rejection of Christian principles by good people of any race.

How would you like to have a congregation of people who are good enough honestly to set out to find the ultimate truth that lies back of this bewildering, measureless

[3] Used by permission of the author and of the *Saturday Review.*

universe? To believe that there is a God may not be very difficult for any person in your church or outside of it, but to trust him is quite another thing. One could hardly think of Jesus going on to the bitter end without trusting that God is the final answer. Paul, too, came to the place where God was something other than part of the thought forms of his day. Man has tried to explain Paul's experience on the road to Damascus, but with little success. But life after that was different. When he asked the question "Who art thou, Lord?" he was conscious of the fact that truth was coming to him in the form of a person, that the Man whom he was persecuting had everything that was necessary to know about God and himself.

It may be harder to believe in God and in a universe that is measured by the yardstick of 150,000,000 light-years to the fartherest known star than it was in Paul's day, but no less important and necessary. It is just too bad if a man does not find something which is able to satisfy his deeply implanted religious faculty. A religion without God is no religion at all. Indeed, the more staggering the universe becomes and the more hopeless seem the conditions, the more necessary it is to have God.

Men may not be Christian according to your theological definition of God and of Christianity. I sometimes find myself wishing we would discard the word "Christianity" and substitute for it the word "Christlikeness." For what about the man whose spirit is reaching out toward God—who is trying his level best, and perhaps asking you to help him, to find life's satisfaction in something other than material values? In fact, goodness belongs to any man, not when he justifies his actions, but when he is dissatisfied with himself, when he has a sense of missing the mark, and when he feels the need of forgiveness and for a life that is fashioned according to the pattern of Jesus Christ.

There may be other marks of a good man, but if Jesus never loses the pattern of compulsion in his life, he is on the way toward becoming a Christlike man. Look, young man, at the faces of people you meet who feel the upward pull toward a higher and better life. When you find them, your heart will rejoice at the opportunity of sowing a seed which will produce a harvest, some sixty, some thirty, and some a hundredfold.

Yes, mankind is your business. It partakes of the nature of the youth in Maurice Hewlett's story in *Pan and the Young Shepherd* who said:

I got up the mountain ledge and from the top saw the world stretched out. . . . and then I thought no more; but my heart leaped to meet the wind, and I ran and ran! I felt my legs under me. I felt the wind buffet, hit me on the cheek. The sun shone. The bees swept past me singing. And I sang, shouted, "World, world, I am coming."

I wish you would look out upon as much of the world as you can see through observation, meeting with other minds and hearts, and through reading. I wish you would expose your heart to its aching need and to the voice of God. Then you will answer, "Listen, world, I am coming to dedicate my life to your desperate needs. "